CONNECTING CONFIDENCE & APTITUDE

Katrin Winkler & Nicola Bramwell ©2021

How to Succeed as
A WOMAN IN LEADERSHIP

Linchpin Books

Cover image courtesy of Shutterstock.
Book layout and cover by Chantal Vandevorst.
Cartoon illustrations by Russell Dean.

ISBN 978-94-6407-544-1
D/2021/15004/03

Linchpin Books is a trade name of The Bayard Holding bv,
Registered in Belgium, No. BE 0629 734 985
www.linchpinbooks.eu

FOREWORD
BY SABINE DECKER, PENTHESILEA CONSULT

Do we really need another book on women in leadership? Yes, we do! Let me explain why. When I started my career some 30 years ago, I was convinced the shining, promising age of women in leadership was just about to begin. All these ambitious, highly educated young women on the edge of breaking into a bright corporate future could no longer be ignored or blocked. Surely, we would be fostered and promoted. My strongest argument, so I thought, was the fact that many young women were daughters of men in senior positions, so supporting and promoting us would come naturally to them. How mistaken I was. In retrospect, I must state disillusionedly, it was a much tougher path than I ever imagined, and support was rare. As a result, apart from a few outstanding 'lighthouse' examples, the corporate world today has still not reached full equality where diversity is wholeheartedly embraced. It means we do still need to discuss women's standing and how to achieve better.

Is this why we need a quota? Again, 30 years ago my answer would have been easy and clear: Of course not! But today? My answer is no longer that straightforward. Looking back at the progress that has been made, I must concede that underlying structural realities still require structural changes. That may unfortunately also have to be imposed from outside. Is it therefore all doom and gloom? Of course not. It is commonly accepted that diverse teams are more successful and that companies acknowledging this fact and acting appropriately show better result. Even more importantly, these companies achieve a competitive advantage in recruiting top talents with their modern and open working environment.

For me and most of my fellow female colleagues with years of experience, we have learned our lessons well. We know how to make ourselves heard and, even more importantly, understood. We are happy with the choices we made throughout our lives and careers, confident in our roles and hopefully being able to be our authentic selves. Was it easy to get there? No, it was not. And I would have appreciated to have had more women as role models for finding my way and for helping and mentoring me through the jungle out there. Therefore, we need books about women in leadership, like this one. This book will you help to understand what is going on in an environment that may be neutral, challenging or at its worst, even hostile. It will help you to understand some rules and give support and guidance on how to find your authentic self. Because only if you are balanced are you able to be a good or even great leader. Leadership is not about giving the right instructions, delegating tasks and getting things done – this is good management. Leadership is much more than that. It is about creating a work environment that let people grow and shine, helping them to develop and making them successful too. After all these years this is my greatest joy. What I find most rewarding is making the people that work with me successful, seeing them grow and prosper. This is also a substantial part of my success.

This book aims to be here to help you on your way, to remind you of the little things that may have slipped your mind and most importantly, to encourage your pursuit of success. It is not only a 'how to...', but will give you a deeper, yet practical understanding of the corporate rules and unwritten rules. If I only would have known all this earlier in my career!

Sabine Decker studied law and began her corporate career in the male dominated German machinery industry in 1992. She has been a board member of a public listed company and started her own consulting and interim management business in 2003. Since then, she has been working on numerous restructuring and transformation projects, both as an adviser and in operational roles.

FOREWORD
EXPERT VIEW BY IAN ROBERTS,
HEAD OF KINGSTON BUSINESS SCHOOL

The distinct challenges that women experience in leadership roles and relationships are serious, important, profound. Too often society throws responsibility for progress back onto the shoulders of individual women: shoulders that often also carry a weight of expectation, frustration, ambition, caring responsibilities and being 'other'. We share the responsibility as society, refusing to pit one side against another and learning from one another. We can lead with grace and be disruptors of our own and others' destiny. While reading this book go and make mischief like Emma Watson!

"Feminism can be humorous, and we all have a different way of approaching that. I often wonder what mischief I can make to spread the word in a playful way. You can't take everything in life seriously, can you?" (Emma Watson, actor and activist).

Ian Roberts is an eminent leadership development and organizational psychology expert. Prior to joining Kingston Business School in London in 2019, he spent his career working with senior executives across the commercial and public sectors to coach, inspire and develop talent and transform organizations.

AUTHORS

Professor Dr. Katrin Winkler is a Human Resources and Leadership professor at the University of Applied Sciences (UAS) Kempten, Germany. As both academic professor and having many years' experience leading international teams and consulting for leaders around the world, she shares her insights on effective leadership and how to motivate and inspire people.

Nicola Bramwell has an MBA and business background in strategic marketing, general management and leadership. She has held senior positions in blue chip companies in complex industries and shares much expertise in leadership, leading change and developing effective communication skills for personal influence.

TABLE OF CONTENTS

Penguins

Have you ever wondered why airports are full of penguins on a Monday morning? To be fair they do vary in colour; some are dressed in black suits, some in dark blue and some in different shades of grey. This procession is usually repeated on Friday night as well, as these early Monday and Friday evening flights are dedicated to commuting managers, consultants, etc, most of whom are men. If you look at senior management meetings you will find the same scenario. Again why? This is how senior managers look. When half the population is female, it is striking that women made up only 7% of the Fortune 500 CEOs in 2020. This was even highlighted as an "all-time record" (1). So how come penguins are so successful?

The discussion about women in leadership is controversial and often ends in assigning guilt to one group or the other, or even in a war of the sexes. This is not what this book is about. We would like to take a pragmatic look at why women don't make it to the top, and at the same time review some ideas on what women can actually do to gain acceptance in this still male dominated business world. We want to point out that a "battle" approach will not get us anywhere (2). We do believe however that women need to open their eyes to understand the world around and how to navigate it. So, we will look at how penguins succeed and what women can also do to achieve success in business and in leadership, and at the same time think about connecting with the male (and female) workplace without bitterness or resentment.

Yes, there are real barriers out there, yet we believe that complaining about a situation and getting "victimitis" has never helped anyone. We can shift the balance as women can also leverage **four elements of leadership**:

1 **Mindset and attitude:** the way we think about others and ourselves has a strong influence on how we behave (3)
2 **Personal presence:** the perception we create of ourselves has a strong influence on how we are seen as a leader (4)
3 **Cognitive dimension:** as not everyone is a natural born leader, a solid understanding of the tools, tasks and skills required to be a leader can focus learning and development (5)
4 **Strong support networks:** how we relate to others and the environment this creates nurtures both ourselves and those around us (6)

As we explore key topics, we will relate to research studies, examples, as well as build stories to anchor key learnings more easily. We also take a humorous approach to a situation which could be described as dire, as the glass ceiling seems to be more stable with fewer and fewer cracks appearing. Based on our experience as leaders who have made it to senior leadership positions, we believe it is possible to shift the scales through overall better connectedness between men and women, understanding the connections between barriers and enablers, and by individual women connecting the pieces together to be great leaders.

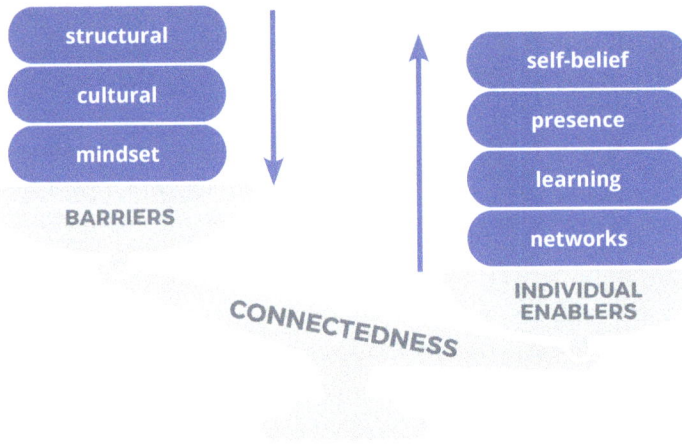

```
┌─────────────┐                    ┌─────────────┐
│  structural │           ↑        │  self-belief │
├─────────────┤           │        ├─────────────┤
│  cultural   │     ↓     │        │  presence   │
├─────────────┤           │        ├─────────────┤
│  mindset    │           │        │  learning   │
└─────────────┘           │        ├─────────────┤
                          │        │  networks   │
   BARRIERS               │        └─────────────┘

                                   INDIVIDUAL
                                   ENABLERS
          CONNECTEDNESS
```

Figure 1: Shifting the scales

The business world needs to care because **diversity works**! Women in particular bring new dimensions to teams and leadership roles. Men and women have different view-points, ideas, and market insights which shape their approach to business. Together we can achieve better problem solving. Gender-diverse teams also provide easier access to resources and a gender-diverse workforce allows a company to serve a diverse customer base better. Companies cannot ignore 50% of the potential workforce or potential custom-ers and expect to be competitive in the global economy. Furthermore, from a leadership perspective, women have been proven to have better emotional intelligence. Research by the Hays Group found that "women outperform men in 11 of 12 key emotional intelligence competencies crucial for effective leadership" and this data came from 55,000 profession-als across 90 countries (7).

> **A diverse workforce allows a company to meet the needs of global business today**

Despite the evidence on why diversity counts and even willingness to overcome lack of gender and other types of diversity, the picture at the top is still limited. Many global companies will look diverse on an aggregated level, however, at senior levels the picture is quite different. There is evidence of a glass ceiling and discrimination due to **institutional barriers** that have to come down. These are both structural, cultural and attitudinal (mindset). There are also **self-imposed barriers** that women must be aware of! Our own mindset or self-belief can be very limiting. Women also fail to speak up and ask for what they need, don't challenge behavioural norms and seldom publicize accomplishments! Women also make choices to work in more positive environments as our personal values can mean we are driven by purpose and a desire to be connected to something bigger than ourselves (8). To shift the balance, women can learn from men and can learn to do things differently to men, even better sometimes.

- Penguins are very good at accepting praise and self-marketing – ask yourself honestly, how would you rate on this?
- Penguins wear the uniform – so if you want to be part of a crowd, you first have to look the part!
- Penguins have a strong tendency to attribute success to their own competencies and efforts, whilst women tend to acknowledge the contributions of others as key to their personal success – so where do you fall? Do you have positive belief in your own capability and accomplishments?
- Penguins naturally build large and broad networks with other penguins. This gives them access to senior penguins and quicker access to information, such as new opportunities. How strong is your network? Do you set goals and are you direct when it comes to asking for help? Do you help others? How good are you at connecting with all types of people?

Yes, we have to be better sometimes and that may not be fair but there are existing orders that are not merit based, hence not fair. To paraphrase a good example, "Ginger Rogers did everything Fred Astaire did – only backwards and in high heels" (9). Especially for women, to be taken seriously as a business partner or not, we are at a disadvantage for simply being female. Research by Catalyst (10) suggested that women leaders who express more "female stereotype behaviour" such as smiling, are considered less competent whereas women who express more "male stereotype behaviour" such as more aggressive behaviour, are considered less likeable. It will always be a balancing act and image counts!

What we can do is choose how we react to current norms, barriers and biases. We can choose how we connect with men and women for joint success. We can choose how we dress and how we address others. We can choose how we use our energies and purpose for personal growth and to create a new and better order, for ourselves, other women and all those around us. We need to be confident in our self and others, have the aptitude to manage and lead, and seek to expand all successes across our growing networks. We may ruffle a few feathers along the way and that can be fun too!

Chapter One

WHY DIVERSITY WORKS (AND MATTERS)

Penguins like to be with other penguins

Penguins (and humans) are social creatures, and this social context continues in the workplace. Our networks and friendships provide legitimacy and group recognition. There is nothing wrong with this and it is natural; penguins and people get along well with those who are like them, share the same values, experiences and backgrounds. Similarity makes us feel safe, comfortable, get agreement and reassurance in our own identity. The scientific term for this behaviour is "similarity attraction" or "love of the same" - which means the tendency of individuals to associate and bond with similar people. In other words, "birds of a feather flock together". It does mean penguins may tend to hire other penguins as it is easier and they think they know what they are getting (11).

Other informal social networks are important for penguins and symbolised by activities such as after work drinks. Many penguins enjoy the after-work camaraderie, and though reasoning for such behaviour may be solidarity, it can leave others feeling excluded. Women often feel unable to attend due to home or life commitments, may not wish to attend based on assumptions of a sexist environment, but also, women are rarely admitted. These "men's clubs" depend on exclusivity and limited access for their power and are associated with promotions from within and providing networking and professional mentoring opportunities that are simply not available to anyone who isn't a part of them (12).

THE PROBLEM WITH SAME

> Similarity attraction risks narrowing the mind and limits options in decision making

For companies to succeed, and be better than the competition, they need to be well positioned to deal with the business world of today, characterized by constant change, globalization, cultural and individual differences. With digitalization making choices ever more accessible, global businesses need to work even harder to win sales, as well as attract good employees. Furthermore, products, services and even strategies can be copied, yet people are unique, and it is the people in a company that provide advantage (13). Investing leadership time on building and empowering teams of diverse workers to perform beyond what is simply expected, drives innovation, growth and competitive advantage.

"WE NEED DIVERSITY OF THOUGHT IN THE WORLD TO FACE THE NEW CHALLENGES."
(Tim Berners-Lee, British physicist and inventor of the World Wide Web)

Stimulating employees to be creative means all possible perspectives, alternative solutions and options are considered in planning and problem solving and decision making. However, two significant challenges to this include groupthink and homogeneous teams.

Groupthink is the exaggerated desire for agreement and harmony that endangers realistic assessments and decision making (14). Though not consequent for all teams, risks increase under pressure and when the group overestimates itself. Decisions are then not questioned, not all relevant information is gathered – especially when the information is not positive, and reflection on different options is missing.

Homogeneous teams may be easy to manage and communication simple, yet this can also result in no new ideas coming to the table and focus remains only on what is already known. It can also be because "agreeing with someone is much less hassle than rejecting their idea head on" (15). The best way to solve these critical issues is by having heterogeneous or diverse teams.

There are many headlines reporting that companies with diverse workforces and diverse management teams outperform competitors that do not (16, 17, 18):
• Diversity unlocks innovation and drives market growth
• Financial successes include increased revenues and higher profit

- Employee satisfaction is improved when people see like-minded role models and company image enhanced with better social responsibility
- Ease of attracting further diverse talents

Yet the question remains – what is the link? Diversity is proven to impact business performance through positive behaviours. First and foremost, making better decisions. Diversity prompts people to analyze facts, think more deeply and develop their own opinions. It improves the way people think and therefore generates better conclusions and results (18). Therefore, diversity is critical in a fast-paced world of continuous innovation and change.

In the context of companies, the term diversity signifies the differences and similarities of the workforce due to inherent or acquired characteristics. Both are important and both areas can be managed. Inherent diversity includes gender, ethnicity, age and disability. Acquired includes learnt skills and knowledge such as languages. The value of inherent diversity can include customer focus, for example, when at least one member of a team has the same traits as the customer, this customer type is better understood by the whole team (16). Companies which commit themselves to diverse leadership are better able to win top talent and improve their customer orientation, employee satisfaction, and decision making. All that leads to a cycle of increasing returns and therefore more success (17).

WHAT WOMEN BRING THAT IS BENEFICIAL TO THE WORKPLACE

Firstly, there are many advantages of gender-diverse teams based on how they work (16, 19):
- Men and women have different viewpoints, ideas, and market insights which shape their approach to business. Together they can achieve better problem solving.
- Gender-diverse teams provide easier access to resources, such as various sources of credit, multiple sources of information, and wider industry knowledge.
- Gender-diverse workforces allow companies to serve a diverse customer base better.

Simply put, companies cannot ignore 50% of the potential workforce or potential customers and expect to be competitive in the global economy.

> "NO COUNTRY CAN TRULY DEVELOP IF HALF
> ITS POPULATION IS LEFT BEHIND."
> (Justine Greening, UK International Development Secretary, 2012-2016)

WOMEN IN LEADERSHIP?

From a leadership perspective, women have been proven to have better emotional intelligence. That means women are better able to understand their own emotions and those of others and better manage responses in social interactions and stressful scenarios. Research by the Hays Group found that "women outperform men in 11 of 12 key emotional intelligence competencies crucial for effective leadership", and their data came from 55,000 professionals across 90 countries (7).

Women demonstrate better self-awareness, empathy, coaching and mentoring, influence, inspiration, conflict management, organizational awareness, adaptability, teamwork and achievement orientation. Women only score slightly higher than men in positive outlook and emotional self-control is the only competency in which men and women show equal performance (7).

As Daniel Goleman, Co-Director of the Consortium for Research on Emotional Intelligence in Organizations at Rutgers University said, "the data suggests a strong need for more women in the workforce to take on leadership roles" (20), because the most effective leaders are those who have the greatest **emotional intelligence** (7). This creates a healthy, more helpful workplace as such leaders can remain calm during times of turbulence. By decoding non-verbal clues, they address and resolve workplace problems or tensions before they escalate. By serving as empathetic mentors and coaches, they nurture the next generation of professionals. By inspiring others, they can positively impact their teams and drive greater performance throughout the organization.

Women have also been shown to have **effective communication skills** such as listening and sharing ideas, and this encourages teamwork and more collaborative work effort, more team spirit. When women manage teams through effective communication and relationship building, they also make teams feel that their efforts and contributions are valued through showing appreciation, and this leads to further increased efforts to benefit the organization. Showing compassion and care really does help to boost productivity and communication is a meta-competency, essential for great leadership (21).

Finally, female leaders **drive change**, both strategic and organizational, another essential leadership competency. Women are willing to redefine culture, setting inclusive policies and leading by example to make change happen. In 2018, Emma Walmsley, new CEO of

GSK, was awarded Britain's Most Admired Leader by business publication, Management Today (22). She defined one element of her own job as "defining and modelling the culture through your own behaviour or the actions you take". Women leaders have actively changed organizational values and policies to increase flexibility, home working and introduce new benefits such as childcare. By leading by example, they shift attitude and mindsets too.

Why do the emotional competencies and communication play such a part in **effective leadership**? It is because leadership is inspiring others to be engaged and committed to work and personal success. It is creating an environment in which others can succeed and going beyond managing tasks to achieving results through people (5).

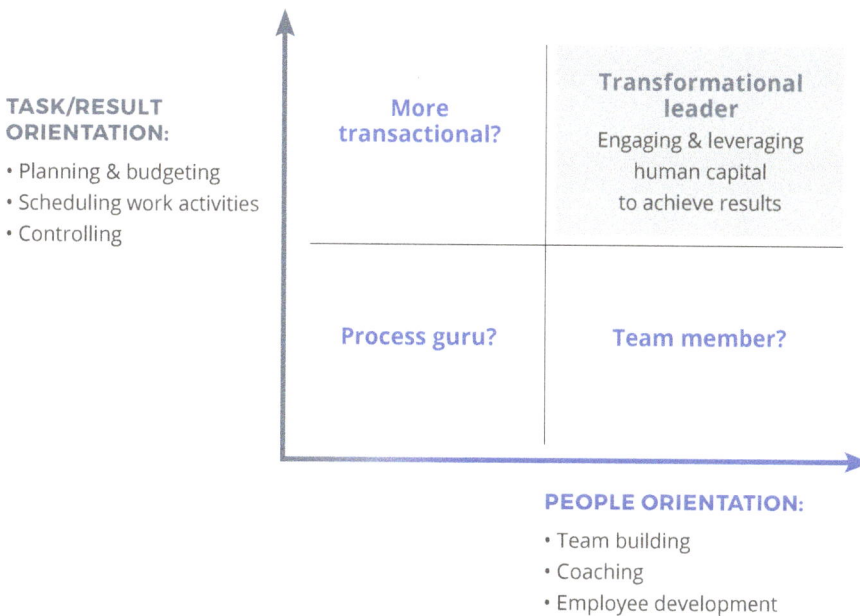

TASK/RESULT ORIENTATION:

• Planning & budgeting
• Scheduling work activities
• Controlling

More transactional?

Transformational leader
Engaging & leveraging human capital to achieve results

Process guru?

Team member?

PEOPLE ORIENTATION:

• Team building
• Coaching
• Employee development

Figure 2: Responsibilities of leadership include tasks and people (23)

The most effective leadership style, **transformational leadership** (5), balances both a focus on business performance (tasks such as planning, scheduling work and controlling) and people-related actions such as team building and coaching. To achieve this, a leader must therefore manage both the organization's needs and ensure the team members understand the organization's purpose. By communicating and involving people, teams feel committed, and this ultimately leads to higher satisfaction levels, motivated employees, and overall better performance (5). To maximize the potential of women in leadership, both men and women must therefore understand how leaders are effective and how to hire, develop, promote and retain such great talent. However, with so much evidence showing what women bring to teams and the benefits of women in leadership roles, why are there so few women in senior roles in global organizations?

> *The best advice I ever received... Sophie Grayson*
> *Keep banging down the doors. Don't just tap on them!*

EVIDENCE OF A GLASS CEILING

In the corporate world, a significant barrier to women making the greatest contribution is their slowed advancement to senior levels. Though companies attempt to reduce bias in hiring and promotions, at the critical step from entry level to management roles, men are still promoted more than women leading to perceptions of unfairness and contributing to the increased gender gap at higher levels.

> **Women are 18% less likely to be promoted to manager than men (24)**

Just looking at US statistics, 52% of the population are female, 57% of college graduates are female and within the corporate world, entry level roles are filled 47% by women. However, the glass ceiling does appear to start immediately. Women in management falls to 37% and tails off to only 20% at C-suite level, and most are in staff jobs that rarely lead to a CEO role. In addition, since the vast majority of CEOs come from senior VP roles, this fall dramatically hurts women's odds of reaching the very top. Hence women making up only 7% of Fortune 500 CEOs in 2020 (1).

CORPORATE PIPELINE

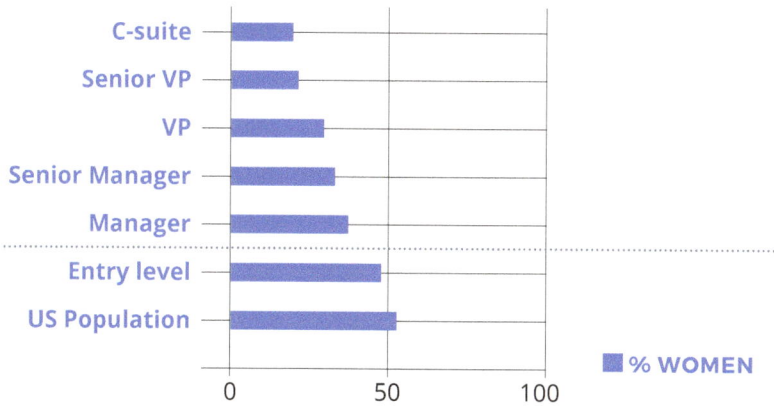

Figure 3: The promotion gap (24)

What research by groups such as McKinsey and the Lean In Organization also shows is that women are not leaving their companies at higher rates than men, and very few plan to leave the workforce to focus on family. It is structural obstacles and mindsets that hold women back. One such example is the perception of the problem that men believe women are well represented in leadership despite data to the contrary (24).

> 50% of men think women are well represented in leadership in organizations where only one in ten senior leaders is a woman. Data from 70,00 employees, McKinsey 2017 (24)

IS IT SIMPLY GENDER DISCRIMINATION?

No, it is not that simple, yet forms of gender discrimination clearly run through the workplace. As shown above, bias in promotion leads to women being less likely to advance to the top of their fields. Salary data also shows women earn about 78 cents on the dollar compared to men in USA (28). Discrimination is defined as treatment or distinction towards a person based on the group to which they are perceived to belong. In many countries, discrimination is illegal. The United Nations defines another more pertinent problem, gender stereotyping.

Gender stereotyping, according to the United Nations, "is a generalised view or preconception about attributes or characteristics, or the roles that are or ought to be possessed by or performed by women and men. It is harmful when it limits women's and men's capacity to develop their personal abilities, pursue their professional careers and make choices about their lives" (26). Both the Office of the United Nations High Commission for Human Rights and the Gender Equality Commission of the Council of Europe (27), state that gender stereotyping can limit the development of the natural talents and abilities of women and men, as well as their educational and professional experiences and life opportunities in general.

Let us consider stereotyping first. **Stereotypes** begin to form early in childhood to serve a purpose for simplification. Clustering people into groups with expected traits does help navigate the world without being overwhelmed by information. The downside is that the potential for prejudice is hard-wired into human cognition. Stereotypes about women both result from, and are the cause of, deeply engrained attitudes, values, norms and prejudices against women. Unfortunately, they can be used to justify and maintain the historical relations of power of men over women as well as sexist attitudes that hold back the advancement of women. Not only can it be seen in statistics, but it can also be observed in the way women are assessed or described.

The challenge of expectations

One example from funding applications to venture capitalists in Sweden highlighted stereotypical ideas about women having **qualities** opposite to those considered important as an entrepreneur. What they found was that the venture capitalists questioned women applicants' credibility, trustworthiness, experience, and knowledge. Where men were described as "young and promising", women were "young, but inexperienced". Where a man was "cautious, sensible and level-headed", a woman was "too cautious and does not dare." As a result, women seeking financial support for new businesses were only given 25% of the applied-for funding, when men received an average of 52% (25).

The challenge of proof

A second example and important concept is the differences in how genders are **assessed** at work. According to human resource theory, performance assessments, such as those most companies undertake annual to measure goals, consider the extent to which a person currently meets the requirements of their role. In other words, it is about looking backwards on historic results, it can be very objective and can show track record. Potential on the other hand is described as the possible ability to perform effectively in other roles or more senior roles. It is a future looking subjective assessment. In best practice, potential should consider ability, engagement and ambition and be evaluated by multiple trained assessors or in assessment centres.

Studies have shown that in hiring or promoting, male potential is preferred over female track record and male job applicants are perceived to have high levels of leadership potential and rated as better employment prospects (30). Such findings provide evidence that women's leadership performance can be overlooked, and potential is not recognized by employers, and this will be a significant barrier to career progression and a detriment to organizations missing excellent candidates. The question becomes, how can such bias be overcome? It starts with understanding the biases.

> **Women are evaluated primarily on performance, while men are often promoted on potential, even over proven female performance. (30)**

THE BROADER PROBLEM OF UNCONSCIOUS BIAS

Believe it or not, our decisions are not always our own thanks to the unconscious biases buried in our brains (5, 17, 31). Examples include:

- Affinity bias is the tendency to favour people who are like us in some way (like penguins). When we gravitate toward people who are like ourselves, we may pay less attention to the people who are not as much like us. This can be a problem if we alienate the people who seem to be less like us and give the impression that we do not value their opinion as highly. Additionally, if we tend to solicit input just from the people who are most like us, we miss opportunities to gain new insights and diverse perspectives.

- Anchoring bias refers to making decisions from the first piece of information that we learn from. That means beware the hasty decisions!
- Confirmation bias can unfortunately reinforce this as once we believe something to be true, we see more evidence that supports it.
- Negativity bias is when our minds react more strongly to negative experiences rather than positive ones, making us more likely to turn down opportunities or new ideas or new people as threats and not consider the potential advantages.
- Frequency illusion. Have you noticed that when you learn a new word you start seeing it everywhere? Our brains have a habit of trying to see patterns, so we notice things more if they are interesting to us.

There are many more examples of such unconscious ways our brains work and as all brains function differently, different people lean more towards different biases. The question is where do they come from and what can we do about them?

Unconscious bias relates to the mental "shortcuts" our brain takes based on personal experiences and stereotypes. So, unconscious biases are the automatic, mental shortcuts used to process information and make decisions quickly.

At any given moment we are flooded with information yet can only consciously process about forty items. Cognitive filters and learning allow the mind to unconsciously prioritize, generalize, and dismiss large volumes of input. These shortcuts can be useful when making decisions with limited information, focus, or time, but can sometimes lead us astray and have unintended consequences in the workplace, meaning we overlook great ideas, undermine individual potential, as well as create a less than ideal work experience for others. However, at the individual level, the extent to which such biases are internalized and acted on varies widely and in complex ways. It is therefore important to know that background, personal experiences, societal stereotypes and cultural context can have an impact on decisions and actions without realizing it.

Yet it gets worse…. Even when we believe we are being rational in our thinking, we can still be misled. Attempts to observe others and their behaviour, free from any interpretation, can be hindered by observational errors. Judgement based on first impressions prevails. We are also prone to logical mistakes such as assuming people who speak well have deep thoughts and the halo effect is the tendency for an impression created in one area to influence opinion in another area – essentially, an overall impression of a person ("he is nice!") impacts evaluations of that person's specific traits ("he is also smart!").

The challenge of a name

As another example, Corinne Moss-Racusin, a social psychologist, showed that unconscious bias can even play a big role in STEM disciplines (science, technology, engineering, and math), despite all scientific objectivity. Her team designed a CV of a job candidate and asked more than 100 STEM professors to assess it. Half of the professors were given the CV with a male name on it ("John"), the other half received exactly the same CV, but from a "Jennifer". The results were surprising. Despite having the exact same qualifications and experience, Jennifer was perceived as significantly less competent. As a result, Jennifer experienced a number of disadvantages that would have hindered her career advancement if she were a real applicant. Because they perceived the female candidate as less competent, the scientists in the study were less willing to mentor Jennifer or to hire her as a lab manager. They also recommended paying her a lower salary, on average, $4,000 per year (13%) less than John (32).

Are you struggling with this depth of unconscious bias? Well, think about a CEO – what image comes to mind?

What probably happened in your mind was this: almost instantly, you had a picture in your head of a tall, European or North American-looking man in a suit....

Or have you ever felt surprised and maybe even a bit uncomfortable after hearing the pilot's voice welcoming you on board of a plane, and realizing that the pilot is a woman?

These are real examples of unconscious bias. It is not that we are bad people, these are examples of the way we **represent word meanings** and our tendency to interpret words by referring to a general idea of the type of thing that this word represents, rather than by using a check-list style definition to think rationally.

IS DIVERSITY ALL ABOUT PROMOTING WOMEN?

Women in the workforce contribute to higher business performance and contribute to the global economy. Female leaders contribute more. Yet, why don't women make more impact at the top? Is it the glass ceiling? Do companies just need to decide to promote women? Do women just need to decide to go for top jobs?

Creating and retaining a diverse workforce, including women at the top, is not about simply "adding" under-represented groups. Firstly, good people are attracted to winning companies, so business success counts when people look to join. Secondly, for women in particular, three other factors are also essential to hire and retain them in an organization.

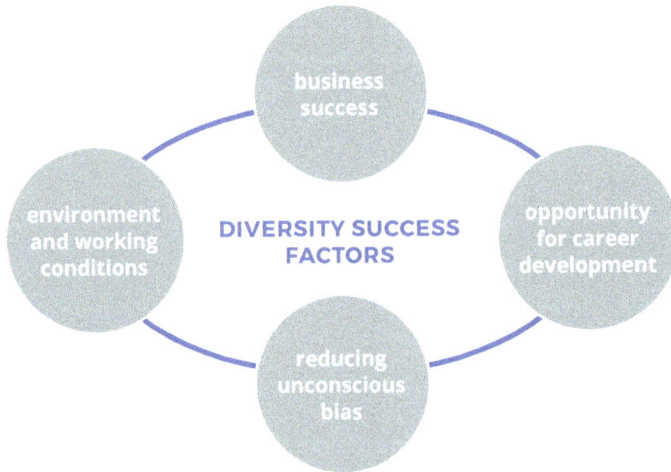

Figure 4: Factors for creating a diverse workforce is multi-faceted (5)

The **environment and working conditions** are important, and corporate values of inclusiveness need to drive policies to ensure women, in particular those with in dual roles (career/household responsibility), remain in the workforce. Women especially join or leave companies for work-life balance. Furthermore, more women leave companies due to politics and the "men's club".

The **opportunity for career development** must also be transparent and fair for all employees. However, there is much evidence showing that although gender neutral opportunity is expected in leading organizations, women's experiences differ widely and are often based on actions from their direct managers.

This links into the final diversity key success factor, **reducing unconscious bias** in managers. As we have discussed, unconsciously, like penguins, we tend to like people who look like us, think like us, come from backgrounds similar to ours. The challenge is therefore clear when so many men sit on boards and in senior roles. This effect can have massive impact on managers hiring and promoting decisions if managers are not actively taking their own unconscious bias into account.

If organizations have no active steps for valuing and leveraging diversity and inclusion, the working environment, opportunity for career development and unconscious bias will always remain institutional barriers to women making more impact at the top of organizations. In "What Works – Gender Equality by Design" Iris Bohnet, a behavioural economist at Harvard, showed that increasing transparency works because "people care about what others think" and holding organizations accountable through disclosure is effective in moving towards better gender equality (33). This also shapes **new social norms** - sharing what others do well and pointing out outliers also alters behaviour.

Creating **new role models** and promoting the success of women has also been shown to affect attitudes, especially of other women. At the University of Washington, changing the decorations in the computer science classroom from Star Trek images to gender-neutral art strengthened the female students' associations between women and careers in computer science (34). This effect also builds on the need to increase the pool of women in such key fields. For example, while a number of industries are showing trends of a growing female workforce, sectors like finance, engineering, and technology still tend to be strongly male dominated. In STEM industries overall, women make up just 24% of the workforce in the USA and less than 15% in the UK, possibly due to the continued stereotype that an interest in "hard science" is unfeminine. Yet with STEM occupations projected to be among the fastest growing and best paid, it's important to close the gender gap here.

Tackling gender bias and creating inclusion continues to require a paradigm shift in most organizations. This means a major change is needed in the concepts and practices of how work is accomplished through inclusion and a diverse workforce. For the inclusion of more women, the shift requires both organizations to remove the stumbling blocks, and for women themselves to engage, build personal skills and bring others along with them on the journey.

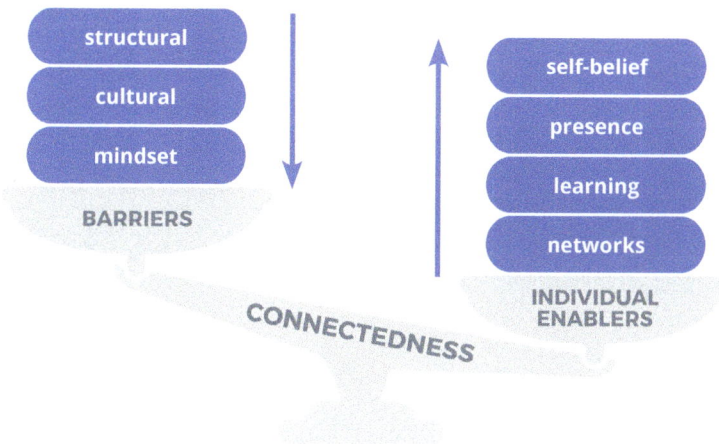

structural
cultural
mindset
BARRIERS

self-belief
presence
learning
networks
INDIVIDUAL ENABLERS

CONNECTEDNESS

Figure 5: Shifting the scales requires organizations to reduce barriers and individual women to leverage the enablers

Organizational diversity requires the removal of structural barriers, cultural change and attitudinal change to overcome the stereotyping that hold women back. As women, we also need to play our part. We will look at the individual enablers in subsequent chapters, yet it must be highlighted that, as women, if we want to enter the room, just tapping at the door doesn't work, we need to bang down the door. However, even if that doesn't work immediately, don't walk away! A key element that limits women detrimentally in the rise to the top is our own beliefs.

"IF YOU ACCEPT A LIMITING BELIEF, THEN IT WILL BECOME A TRUTH FOR YOU."

(Louise Hay, motivational author, 1926-2017)

KEY LEARNING POINTS ON THE VALUE OF DIVERSITY

- Diversity counts! Not just gender, but ethnicity, sexual orientation, social background..... Valuing difference is about integrity and having strong moral principles
- Companies with diverse workforces and diverse management outperform those that do not in terms of growth, profitability, talent attraction and employee satisfaction
- Diverse teams demonstrate better decision making and problem solving
- Homogeneous teams lead to stagnation and no new ideas emerging
- Women in teams add different perspectives and insights
- Women in leadership show better communication skills and drive more strategic and organizational change
- Women have been proven to demonstrate better emotional intelligence competencies crucial for effective leadership

Chapter Two

SELF-IMPOSED BARRIERS FOR WOMEN IN LEADERSHIP

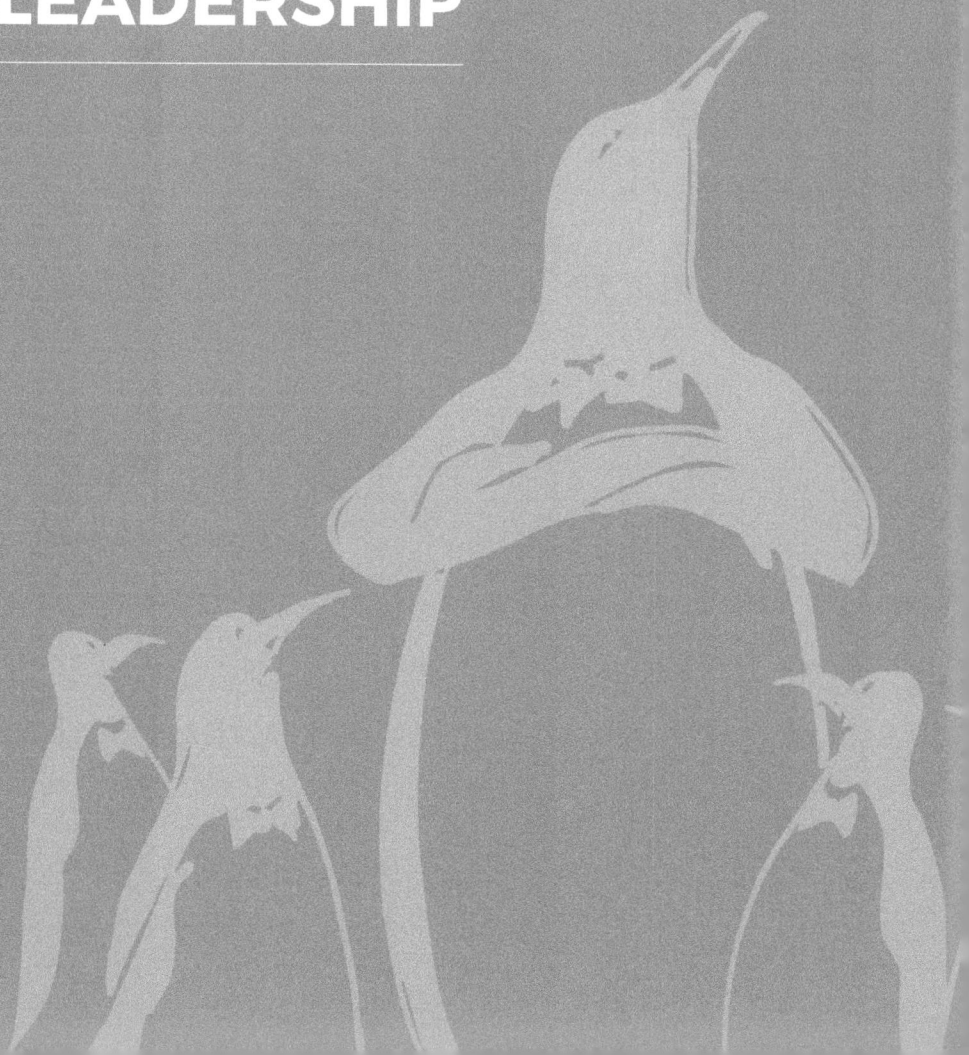

Penguins like power

A penguin's identity is a complex mix of hierarchic groups, tribes, geography and history, and even down the pecking order, lower penguins benefit from the patriarchy at the top (35). The result is an overdeveloped sense of entitlement. They dominate the upper echelons of society in government, in boardrooms, in the media etc etc. Male dominance was born in a time when physical strength trumped wisdom, sensitivity and intelligence, yet this instinct to feel superior continues and the willingness to take on power is linked to deep confidence.

A study to assess confidence differences asked women and men to rate their performance after a maths test. Women overestimated their score on average 15%. The problem was men overestimated their scores by 30% (35).

IT STARTS WITHIN

The way we think about ourselves influences our behaviour and this can be seen by comparing the difference between women who have made it in the "men's world" and women who have opted out (36). Self-efficacy and belief in one's own success and competence are evident in women that persist. Women who do not make it show a stronger tendency for self-doubt and lack of confidence.

> ## "THE OUTSIDE WORLD IS CONSTANTLY TRYING TO CONVINCE YOU YOU'RE NOT ENOUGH. BUT YOU DON'T HAVE TO TAKE THE BAIT…"
>
> (Oprah Winfrey, media proprietor, talk show host, actress, producer, philanthropist)

Such effects of women's own mindsets are factors in why we are under-represented at the very top. There are three parts that we need to acknowledge, understand, and reflect upon before we complain about institutional barriers and biases (7, 29, 34, 37, 38, 39, 40):
• Our own personal mindsets
• Our own unwillingness to speak up
• Our own choices

> *The best advice I ever received… Rose Grayson*
> *You decide who you are and what story you want to tell.*

PERSONAL MINDSET BARRIERS

Examples of the limiting ways women think can be seen specifically in:
• How women under evaluate their own competence
• Stick too rigidly to guidelines
• Fearing failure
• A decline in ambition levels or acceptance of situations that limits ambition

Our **mindset** is all about the assumptions, methods, or notions we hold. In other words, our attitude. As a rule, attitude is a settled way of feeling or thinking about something or someone (4). It can often be something we forgot to re-evaluate and where we lose objectivity despite the evidence around us. Most women are their own worse critics!

Dr Boyatzis, Professor at Case Western Reserve University states that "historically, there has been a **tendency for women to self-evaluate themselves as less competent**, while men tend to overrate themselves in their competencies," yet "the reality is often the opposite" (65).

This also impacts what jobs women apply for. While both genders browse for jobs similarly, we apply for them differently. Women believe they need to meet 100% of the criteria, while men apply after meeting only 60%, hence, as women, we screen ourselves out and end up applying for fewer jobs (37, 40). Fear of repeated failure also means we tend to stop applying for role types once rejected, not because we lack confidence, but we feel we wouldn't be truly valued at the highest levels of the corporate world (38).

And as we age (and get wiser), our desire to move on to the next level also dissipates faster than men's. Though some women never lose real belief in their abilities, as the odds of getting ahead can be perceived to be too daunting, then many bow out. Especially when women miss role models, feel excluded from informal networks and do not have upper management sponsors, it is often easier to do something else. It is tough to bang down all the doors. It's tougher when the penguins only need to tap on the door to get in. We need to be mentally tough to keep going.

Anna's story

"When I was a junior project manager working for a large American consulting firm, I became aware that after two years tenure, others around me where getting involved in larger global projects, whereas mine remained small and very regional. All my projects were delivered on time and on budget and many clients gave me great feedback. After another year in the job, I decided to sit down with my manager to enquire what I needed to do better to be considered for more challenging and more exciting assignments. My manager gave me positive feedback once again on my performance. When I pushed on doing more, she said she was surprised as I had never mentioned new work or promotion even. She assumed I was not interested, and I had assumed if I were good enough, she would have asked me. My first international project was 18 months in Brazil and one of the best experiences professionally and personally."

The issue for Anna? Assumptions constrain the way we think
One difficulty is that in our imagination, when we think about problems or reaching goals, we form patterns. These patterns are self-imposed boundaries or barriers, that keep our thinking in a framework. We constrain our own thinking in this way (41).
This "box" in our head represents our assumptions and we all have assumptions about the way something is or the way something should be. Thinking outside the box is an-

other term for examining and challenging our assumptions and judgements we make every day. We need to have a close look at our assumptions, or those of others, to avoid being guided by them.

Examples for assumptions are:
- *"She has two small kids, she won't have time to be involved in the project"*
- *"He is an introvert. I doubt, he'll be a good leader"*

Leaders especially must question assumptions and also challenge employees to think outside the box in their head. The next time you catch yourself making a judgement about a person's background or working style, stop and ask yourself if this attribute could also be an asset.

THE WOMEN DON'T ASK PHENOMENON

There are many personal and societal reasons why women seldom ask for what they need, want or deserve (39) and this impacts the following:
- Not negotiating for advantage
- Failure to break childhood conditioning
- Unable to challenge behavioural norms
- Not publicizing accomplishments

The second key self-imposed barrier relates to women not asking. Speaking up, asking for what you want or negotiating for advantage differs significantly by gender for both pay and promotions (39). For example, when men are unhappy with pay, they are more likely to fix their unhappiness by asking. Women worry more about the impact of their actions on relationships, causing them to change behaviour – such as asking indirectly, asking for less than they want or trying to be more deserving by working harder to be given what they want without asking. Women also take a more collaborative approach to find solutions that benefit both parties.

Women hesitate before asking for what they want because of gender-based standards of behaviour. In western culture, women are taught that pushing on their own behalf is un-feminine, unattractive, unwelcome and ineffective. Women who are in or want to position themselves for leadership roles also feel they come under different scrutiny. Where men may be encouraged to be ambitious or assertive, women are programmed from a young age not to be "bossy". This means the same behaviours and characteristics—initiative, passion, and taking charge—can be interpreted differently in men and women in the workplace. Research also shows that women leaders who express more "female stereotype behaviour" such as smiling, are considered less competent whereas women who express more "male stereotype behaviour" such as more aggressive behaviour, are considered less likeable (10). It is a very challenging and very unfair double bind.

Finally, women also expect life to be fair. Examples include hoping hard work alone will earn us the recognition and reward we deserve. Women also bide their time and assume they will be invited to participate if they are valued. Women need to speak up, share opinions, give expert advice and publicize accomplishments.

Elizabeth's story

"When I was promoted to vice president of my company I was thrilled as I was the first leader to hold such a title. Six months later at a large company meeting, another colleague was invited up on stage as he too was given a VP title. He however was acknowledged in front of the whole company, presented with a bottle of vintage Krug and, I discovered later, given a significant pay rise. When I approached HR about having no received no pay rise on my promotion, I was told it had not been budgeted and I should be happy to have been rewarded with the title."

The issue for Elizabeth? *How to address and readdress concerns*
In the book, "Women Don't Ask: Negotiation and the Gender Divide" (39), the authors suggest that women's socialization into passive roles is one of the reasons they do not succeed to higher management positions, and they believe that having the skill to ask questions and readdress ideas in a constructive manner is a key learning point.

Preparing to ask for fair pay must be approached in an assertive, friendly and considerate manner. Having a conversation with your manager starting "hi, I need to talk to you about my salary; is now a good time?" is a respectful opener versus "I need more money, or I am leaving". It is important to have information and ideas, yet a non-threatening manner works better for women, when combined with not backing down or giving in (39).

Even when conversations go wrong or take an unexpected direction, the ability and willingness to use questions is a key skill (4). For example, if an idea of yours was dismissed, it is possible to use questions to readdress topics and continue dialogue, whilst still treating others with respect. By listening to the arguments of others, it acknowledges the legitimacy of other's opinions. By accepting common points, neutral ground can be established, or you may even find ways to refocus on their interests. The point is how you approach such discussion to pave the way for further dialogue. Starting with "I would like to discuss the idea with you again" may get you a direct "absolutely not!", however, don't shout or get emotional or back down, change the tone. "I know you hated the idea as it may create a problem for you with ...." Could be seen to acknowledge their strong feelings and show you have listened and are trying to see their view. "What is the concern you have about....?" is a way of reframing into understanding someone else's needs and getting more information and moving away from an argument.

"Now I understand your reaction, yet we need to .... Do you have any ideas about how I could achieve that without creating the ...problem?" This can be seen to be moving around their position and promoting mutual cooperation and problem solving.

Although you may not always achieve the outcome you want, asking in a professional way protects any relationship and improves understanding. It is also a vital skill for women in the workplace.

MAKING CHOICES

For many women, "having it all" is the seemingly impossible dream, meaning combining professional achievement and personal fulfilment can be a struggle. It often leads to women making choices that work for them:

- Choosing to emphasize making a difference rather than focus on title
- Seeking satisfaction in life, not working 100 hours per week...
- Choosing people versus politics
- Creating careers outside of large corporations

Jamie's story

"Eight years ago, I had the idea to create a virtual law firm ... because I felt frustrated with the often toxic nature of law firm culture and I was unable to find a work environment that matched my values" (42).

The issue for Jamie? Lack of desire to compete or win at any cost.
When we don't want to fight the old norms, we can make positive choices to create a

new environment based on different values. Whereas men value power, status and winning significantly more than women, women value relationships, teams and collaboration more (5). This puts our emphasis on group results, team success and the concern for others, even to the point of avoiding confrontation. It has been shown that not only do women modify their behaviour in public, we also shy away from competition with men. Competing is often defined as a male trait and society even allows demonstration of male superiority over women, making the connection that this can't be a woman's domain (39). The result is observed in women downplaying accomplishments so not to intimidate men. It is also seen in a more social style of interaction. This is not a bad thing! Great communicators for instance have the intention to connect with and engage someone else, not make their point or simply try to win (4). Successful organizations are built on trust, and this starts with how we communicate and influence others and how we make others feel (4). It all goes back to the old African proverb, "if you want to go fast, go alone. If you want to go far, go together".

The third element of internal mindset relates specifically to choices women make and diversity at the top of large corporations may be limited as women choose to stay put in less senior jobs if they derive a sense of meaning from their work and have opportunity to pursue greater satisfaction across all parts of their lives (not only family). Women pour energy into making a difference, working with close colleagues and many will not trade that for energy-draining meetings and corporate politics. For a growing number of women, the fastest route to leadership is launching their own business. In the United States, the number of women-owned businesses have increased 74% over the past 20 years, 1.5 times the national average (43). The start-up culture empowers women to be their own boss and pay their own salary, defining how they want to work and making the balance of career and life easier. Running their own company also offers the opportunity for women to collaborate with and hire other ambitious, like-minded women, fostering a new generation of women in leadership.

> ## "LIFE IS A MATTER OF CHOICES, AND EVERY CHOICE YOU MAKE MAKES YOU."
> (John C. Maxwell, leadership author)

Yes, it is not fair and yes, there are real barriers out there, and yes women need to work harder to overcome these, and yes, we have to be honest with ourselves about our own imposed limits. However, we can shift the balance as we can **leverage the four individual enablers** (see figure 5) to develop **four elements of leadership**:

1 **Self-belief** works on **mindset and attitude** to impact the way we think about ourselves and how we behave (3)
2 **Presence** allows us to work on our **professional persona** to create a positive perception of how we are seen as a leader (4)
3 **Learning** expands the **cognitive dimension** to ensure we understand the tools, tasks and skills required to be a leader (5)
4 **Networks** provide **strong supportive environments** to nurture both us and those around us (6)

How to grow and develop in all these four areas is covered in detail in subsequent chapters.

KEY LEARNING POINTS ON SELF-IMPOSED BARRIERS

- The way women think about themselves can cause self-imposed barriers or self-preserving choices that limit career progression to the highest levels in the corporate world

- Our mindset is our own attitude, our assumptions about something or someone. How we think about ourselves, or others, can be a hindrance if we do not challenge our own thinking

- As women, we are often our own worst critics, and we underestimate our own competence and value

- Women are known to be reluctant to step forward due to fear of failure, not wanting to be seen to break the rules or not wishing to be seen to be stepping outside current accepted norms of "female" behaviour

- Women have a tendency to be satisfied with less or with what we have been offered, we show less sense of entitlement and we certainly do not speak up enough about what we need and rarely feel comfortable asking for what we want

- Yet, women more often than not do not accept the politics or battles encountered daily and choose instead to work in more positive environments or focus on broader work/life satisfaction. This can result in women choosing to remain in lower-level roles than capability would suggest, or stepping out of the corporate world all together

- The good news is that we can also choose any route we like and we can choose to be great as a leader by developing ourselves and those around us

Chapter Three

OVERCOMING THE STRUCTURAL BARRIERS

Penguins like today's corporate world

Penguins, in general, are comfortable with the status quo. Penguins have ruled for the last 10,000 years or so. The workplace is based on a male model of work and male code of behaviour (44). Too many businesses remain hierarchic with command-and-control functions. The result is a highly competitive work environment that rewards speed in decision making, individual performance and goal achievement.

Men and women value some of the same aspects of work, such as performance and goal achievement, however rank other aspects differently. Men value power and authority highly; women value relationships, fairness and collaboration (5). The emergence of such gaps only becomes reality after educational settings. Many students encounter real team spirit and sharing during studies, yet once in the corporate world, men adapt to the competitive reality better, leaving women still hankering for genuine collaboration again (44).

ORGANIZATIONAL CHANGE REQUIRED

Penguins may not think much about colony function and structure, yet for humans, especially women, being in the right environment counts. If you don't believe us, read any magazine article on sexual fantasies…. Men will describe the physical activities; women will be imagining the most romantic setting ever! Enough said.

In this chapter we want to highlight how structural barriers in organizations can be overcome. We are very aware that many individuals may not be in a position to impact such changes; however, it is important though to understand how change can occur or what to look for when you are seeking new employment.

For significant and rapid change to occur, a paradigm shift, in other words an essential change in thinking and acting, is required for fully inclusive organizations. Such a paradigm shift requires a sense of urgency, vision for an organization, plans and actions, targets, transparency and accountability. How can this happen? It has to start with awareness, dialogue, commitment and actions towards conscious inclusion. To achieve this, it means building the desire, insight and capacity of people to make decisions with the conscious intent of gender equality.

"IF YOU DO NOT INTENTIONALLY INCLUDE, YOU UNINTENTIONALLY EXCLUDE."

(Neil Lenane, Business Leader of Talent Management)

In forward-thinking organizations, gender equality is becoming a matter of policy, with commitment to equitable gender representation, inclusive company culture, and work-life balance. The key here is use of both equality and equity as two strategies to produce fairness.

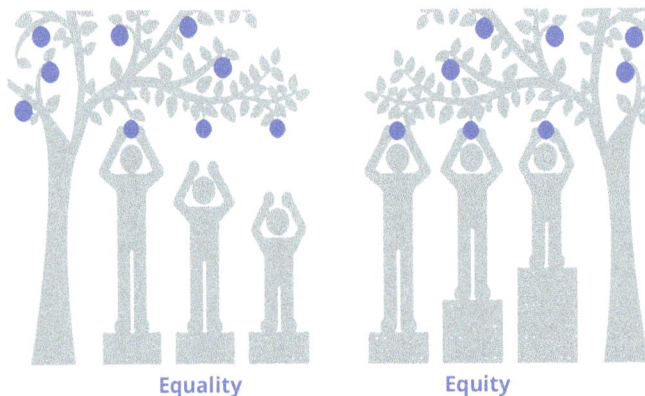

Equality   Equity

Figure 6: Equality and equity are required to overcome structural barriers

Equality is treating everyone the same and aims to promote fairness, but it can only work if everyone starts from the same place and needs the same help. **Equity** is giving everyone what they need to be successful.

First and foremost, the key success factors are around creating a more diverse and inclusive environment overall, improving career development opportunities and challenging bias. However, for any paradigm shift or massive organizational change, there needs to be a sense of urgency, a vision, plans to redefine policies and procedures, and plans to ensure people buy-in. Focus on results is key and achievable through setting targets, ensuring full transparency, and holding all leaders accountable. And this change needs to happen today because it makes business sense to leverage the abilities of female leaders and because the social environment and desire for gender equality demands it. Businesses that fail to see this as an opportunity for competitive advantage will suffer. As Jack Welch said, "if the rate of change outside, exceeds the rate of change inside, the end is in sight".

SETTING THE CHANGE AGENDA

Based on many years or research by the non-profit Lean In organization (45) and others, it is clear that companies need a comprehensive top-to-bottom plan for supporting and advancing women, starting with making a compelling case for gender diversity translated to actions through policies and procedures and tackling gender bias head on. It can even mean redefining company values and a vison to encompass inclusivity.

Examples of ways companies have changed include appointing a diversity officer to shape strategy, plans and measurements. Also, allowing employees to self-select as diversity ambassadors to create movement from within is powerful for wider engagement and bottom-up action as those that want to see change are empowered to do so (24). Investing in employee training on topics ranging from understanding unconscious bias to anti-harassment and how to work in diverse teams facilitates broader development. Training also raises awareness, builds dialogue and gives managers especially the means to drive change. Learnings also show that the journey requires CEO leadership. Getting more men invested also pays off. When direct managers place a high priority on gender diversity, employees are more likely to be committed themselves and when managers offer guidance on how to improve gender diversity, so that it goes from a general policy to something more concrete and actionable, other men are more likely to get on board.

The opportunity seen at Salesforce

An example of a company that has taken such actions successfully is Salesforce, the cloud computing company based in San Francisco (46, 47). CEO Marc Benioff believes that much of a company's culture stems from "the tone from the top," and his commitment began with a conscious effort to address gender diversity when he noticed there were no women in the room at a leadership meeting.

Other actions included:
- Setting goals set to achieve 30% women in senior roles, at senior meetings and in development programs
- Gender neutral development investment for men and women
- Developing talents from within, not just hiring from outside
- Mentorship and championing of women to increase exposure to senior leaders
- Active back to work management after parental leave
- Active challenging of unconscious bias including using internal managers as trainers.

By 2017 Benioff claimed "Diversity is an important part of our culture ... Our employees are telling us that they want to work for a company that cares about diversity..."

As further evidence of commitment, Salesforce spent $3 million in 2015 to close a gender and racial pay gap. And in 2016 the company checked for differences again and due to significant acquisitions found new gaps and spent another $3 million to raise pay for 11% of its 26,000 employees. Now it checks for differences regularly.

"I don't expect politicians to change the world," Benioff said. "I expect all of us to change the world."

> **But what about the "women don't ask" phenomenon? Equity elements that need further consideration:**
> - **Missing role models – women need other women to look to as an example to be emulated.**
> - **Women not self-promoting – structured talent management programs need to seek out and develop all those with potential, not just those who shout the most.**

Active consideration of this barrier needs to be built in to plans and relates to equity elements of gender strategies. With missing female role models in senior leadership roles, women will continue to be influenced by the perception of lack of opportunity. Appointing senior women is a significant and visible signal within an organization. Alongside the unwillingness of women to self-promote and ask for career progression, companies must be bold and seek out talented women, as companies like Salesforce have done.

BUILDING AND RETAINING HETEROGENEOUS TEAMS

Building and retaining heterogeneous teams is aimed at creating the environment and working conditions for inclusivity. Here, substantive actions are often linked to HR policies and procedures such as transparent hiring and recruitment designed to encourage all applicants and discouraging or circumventing bias. As companies lose too many employees in dual roles, policies to retain all types of workers, especially women, need to be in place and can include maternity benefits, back to work programs and flexible working to achieve better work / life balance. Effective application of agile work methods with project-based teams set up on expertise can also focus managers and employees on contribution and away from formal hierarchic limitations.

Examples of actions include strict recruitment with criteria-based hiring and job descriptions with non-biased language, alongside blind resume reviews to reduce gender bias. When looking to retain women, tracking assignment of high-visibility projects and representation by level also improves team mix. Again, work/life balance is improved by allowing homebased working at least 1 day per week, extended maternity cover and even on-site childcare.

Though many companies are more conscious of fairer recruitment, the long-term challenge is maintaining a culture of inclusivity every day. Policy must be followed by consistent behaviour, for example, part-time workers cannot be frowned upon or denied high-visibility projects based on their hours of work. In today's global and post-pandemic world, a 9-5 mindset no longer applies and concerns about lack of work / life balance frequently impacts the ambition of women to be top executives.

> Regarding the "women don't ask" phenomenon? Equity elements that need further consideration:
> - Checking every box – how to keep forms simple and focused on the "must haves"
> - Valuing performance and potential for women

Equity elements of gender strategies must specifically consider how to encourage women to apply for roles, especially at management levels. Because women want to check every box before they apply, being thoughtful about what is put in job postings is important. Avoiding endless lists of requirements, nice-to-haves and strict seniority demands increases female applicants. Furthermore, valuing the performance and proven track record of women is a start, as well as considering potential to lead. It can no longer be acceptable that men are hired on potential yet "when performance is observable, successful women are rated as less likeable that men" (10). Avoiding bias in recruitment promotion may require "blind" applications or objective assessment centres even.

The opportunity of workforce diversity at Starbucks

Starbucks has gone to great lengths to ensure their employees are heard and respected. They have clearly defined diversity policies that reverberate through every aspect of their organization. They also provide access to data in a very transparent way.

It all starts from the pledge, that "we are on a journey to advance racial and social equity for our partners (employees), our community and our society" (48) and "the way we hire, develop and advance our partners (employees) is critical to our journey toward inclusion, diversity and equity at Starbucks" (49).

Policies, programs and initiatives include (48):
- Foundational Inclusion and Diversity learning modules for partners
- Anti-bias content into all hiring, development, and performance assessment toolkits

- Tools for internal talent advancement and opportunities
- Mentorship programs
- Network development and recognition programs across all networks, including an Inclusion and Diversity Virtual Leadership Summit in Q2 FY21
- Transparency in goal setting and progress

Published results 2020 include (49):
- Global workforce 31% male, 69% female
- 100% pay equity in USA, including women and BIPOC (black, indigenous and people of colour)
- 98% median pay for women globally
- 53-65% mix of white workers across all functions globally (retail, manufacturing and corporate)

EXECUTIVE DEVELOPMENT

Achieving more women in leadership goes beyond creating a more inclusive environment to retain women, it also must look at improving career development opportunities. And though companies attempt to reduce bias in hiring, this needs to also be applied to promotions. As discussed in chapter 1, at the critical step from entry level to management roles, men are still promoted more than women leading to perceptions of unfairness and contributing to the gender gap above. Talented women must be promoted to every management level and be prepared for senior roles through systematic executive development.

Critical here is the opportunity for growth, linked to a transparent talent strategy and supported by managers. Tools can include training and personal development, job rotation or expansion, and involvement in key projects. However, surveys show woman have less access to senior management and miss essential mentorship that men have (24), and women experience many companies as unfair in systematic advancement.

Actions top companies have taken include setting targets for women in development programs and senior roles. For example, going back to the Salesforce example, when Salesforce began diversity initiatives, CEO Marc Benioff set 30% goals for women in senior meetings, programs and roles. Salesforce also invested from within rather than hiring from outside (46). In addition, many women hone their knowledge and expertise through business degrees. Business qualifications offer a valuable platform for women to become subject-matter experts, practice leadership skills, and gain the confidence they need to step into senior roles. This also aids credibility!

For executive development programs to work, must have actions include addressing systematic imbalances, with opportunities being seen to go to the most deserving. Promotions must be based on fair and **objective criteria** and women must be seen to move from entry level to manager roles. Such promoting from within is also a positive signal to an organization that inspires and motivates others. This also requires that managers value diversity and be active in the career development of team members. McKinsey data shows that managers' actions have a big impact, both on a woman's career progression and on levels of ambition (24). Women are more likely to be promoted when managers **advocate** for them, give them stretch assignments, and advise them on how to advance. Women who receive advice and interact regularly with senior leaders are more likely to aspire to be a top executive. However, data highlights that women are less likely to receive such mentoring (50).

The opportunity to get more women into leadership positions at Lilly (51)

In 2015, the global pharmaceutical company Lilly, realizing women were not represented in leadership positions at the same rate as men, took actions to rectify this. They ensured buy-in from the top, created transparency and goals, and revamped their talent management and training.
Steps included:
- Training to help managers lead more inclusively by valuing differences, recognizing and overcoming bias, and fostering a speak-up culture
- Talent management processes were changed to minimize unconscious and conscious biases in hiring, management and promotion practices
- In addition, and based on their evidence of "relationship capital" seen in promotions (who you know and trust) and evidence that women were more likely to focus on doing the work itself than on networking and therefore missed opportunities for promotions, they also introduced a Women's Network to groom women for leadership positions. The network augmented the skill development programs with regular events and conferences.

According to lilly.com (2021) women now hold 46% of global management roles and the company was one of four to receive the global Catalyst Award in 2019 for diversity.

> But what about the "women don't ask" phenomenon? Equity elements that need further consideration:
> - Asking for support or advice
> - Negotiating salary – equal pay should be a given...

When considered alongside the "women don't ask" phenomenon, overcoming this barrier requires investment in formal mentoring, even going as far as **sponsorship** of women, particularly by influential male leaders, to helping aspiring women gain the perspective and connections needed to take on larger roles and advance their careers. Yes, women must advocate for themselves if they want to move their careers forward, but to succeed, we can't do it alone. This is also true when it comes to negotiating salary as most women don't and even those that try are not as successful as men. With recent publicity on gender pay gaps, companies must look at fair pay and pay adjustments to eliminate this clear discrimination.

WHAT ABOUT QUOTA?

As organizations begin to track gender by level, external hires, promotions, attrition, assignment and salary comparisons, to achieve genuinely inclusive workplaces, several other options can be considered.

Those in favour of **quotas** believe quotas can enforce the concept of diversity top down and that quotas are not discriminatory but rather compensate for an already existing discrimination. On the other side of the argument, quotas can be seen as discriminatory provoking a conflict between principle of equality; they may reduce employee engagement due to perceptions of unfairness and they can undermine the quality arguments, with further potential stigma for women elected through quotas.

Many governments are introducing more **legislation** related to equality, yet experience is yet to show real impact and early reactions are more related to headline-grabbing statistics rather than actions. For example, the UK Gender Pay Gap Reporting introduced in 2017, reported a 17.4% mean hourly Rate Gap between men and women which remained until 2020 when it fell slightly to 15.5% (52). When assessed at job level, gaps often fell to zero and the headline simply reflected company structures with more men at the top.

So, what about achieving inclusion by **hiring in**? Unfortunately, simply increasing diversity by hiring in is not the solution, especially for senior management. Often the external talent pool is just as limited. This highlights once again that leveraging an internal talent pool is wise, though slower and requires investment in development and preparing potential leaders for senior roles. It necessitates retaining diverse workers at all levels and requires opportunities and actions today, for tomorrow.

We certainly believe that fixes will include a mix of all of the above. It needs policies and procedures for fairness and enhanced equity steps to level the playing field. Change will also only occur when women choose to stay in the game and make change from within. Companies need to take decisions based on their unique environment but the overall intention to include points to the fact that valuing diversity and women in leadership is a mindset leaders must have.

KEY LEARNING POINTS ON STRUCTURAL BARRIERS

- Even in the 21st century, structure barriers hinder the progression of women in many business environments

- For some, significant organizational change is required to achieve conscious inclusion

- Steps to inclusion involve increasing understanding of the issues and leadership from the top to show intent and commitment to equality and equity

- Equality is treating everyone the same to promote fairness. Equity is giving everyone what they need to be successful and this is essential as the diversity playing field is not even today

- Enlightened organizations plan and implement change, build and retain heterogeneous teams and prepare women for senior roles through development, mentoring and sponsorship

Chapter Four

OVERCOMING "THE MEN'S CLUB" (CULTURE AND MINDSET)

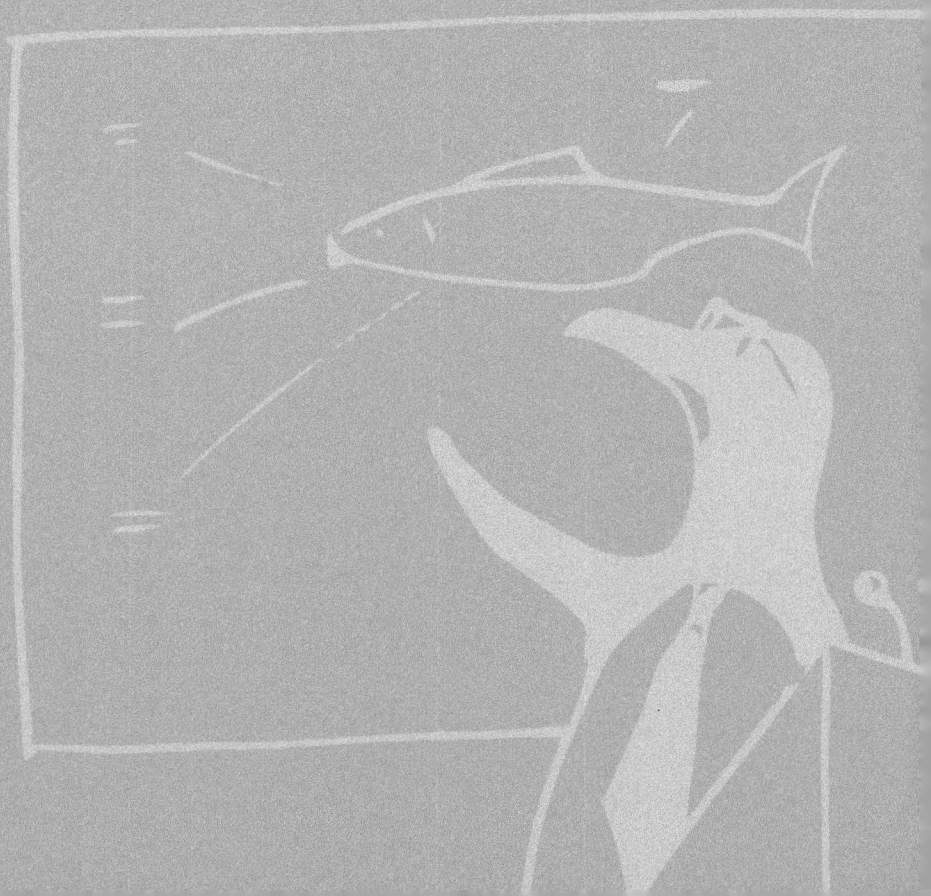

Penguins like to seize the stage

Penguins like their world and they like to offer their opinions whether asked for or not. Especially in groups of other senior penguins, they make statements without considering if they are suitable or valuable or new. Penguin attitude is direct and self-belief tells them that their view is important and therefore others will listen.

What can we learn from this? As women tend more towards an underestimation of our own capabilities, we also create a self-fulfilling prophecy. When we do not talk about our abilities or fail to speak up in groups as we question the value of our inputs first, this lack of contribution may mean we might also be perceived as less capable... Often our own attitude or belief system hinders us, so we are not even seen! You have a voice, so use it. Consider your inputs valuable, then others will too! Be seen at the table or seize the stage too.

UNDERSTANDING WHAT IS NOT WRITTEN DOWN

Women do not simply opt out of the workforce as most cannot afford to. Like men, women leave specific jobs for personal achievement, more money and more recognition. However, more women leave companies due to the "men's club". Furthermore, women pour energy into making a difference, working with close colleagues and many will not trade that for corporate politics. Both the men's club and politics are examples of **corporate culture.**

So, what is culture and how can it be so significant in a business? Culture refers to the way of life, especially the general customs, beliefs and social behaviour of a particular group of people or society, transmitted through **social learning**. This is also closely linked to **individual mindset** as mindset is all about the assumptions, methods, or notions we hold. In other words, our attitude. As a rule, attitude is a settled way of feeling or thinking about something or someone.

In business, the attitude of leaders and the culture of the company shape context. The culture describes how things are done there, the environment and the experiences employees have because it encompasses values and behaviours of that organization. In fact, culture is so important that leading management consultant Peter Drucker famously said, "culture eats strategy for breakfast", meaning that a powerful and empowering culture was a surer route to organizational success.

There are three levels of organizational culture (53):
* Artefacts and symbols mark the surface of the organization, the visible elements such as logos, architecture, organizational structure, processes and even corporate clothing. These are not only visible to the employees but also visible and recognizable for external parties.
* Espoused values contribute to the development of normal standards of the organization for how it conducts business. They concern standards, corporate values and rules of conduct. How the organization expresses and supports strategies, objectives and philosophies.
* Basic underlying assumptions are deeply embedded in the organizational culture and are experienced as self-evident and unconscious behaviours and they are hard to recognize from within. It is these underlying assumptions and behaviours that are not written down which are the most difficult to change.

HOW DO WOMEN PERCEIVE THE MEN'S CLUB?

As mentioned in chapter 1, penguins like being with other penguins and the "men's club" or "boy's club" is part of this social legitimacy, solidarity and group recognition. These clubs depend on exclusivity for their power and women are rarely admitted.

Men and women experience organizational culture differently. For women, these masculine clubs are associated with group activities unrelated to everyone's defined jobs; in other words, the after-work drinks, golf weekends etc. Glimpses into these events suggests a toxic environment such as sexist humour. The outcome of such events includes biased networking which facilitates promotions and inaccessible mentorship opportunities for those not invited along or with limited access. The office "water cooler" used to be a place where co-workers gathered to share advice and ideas, yet it may be more off site now or even online. During these social engagements, work talk is included in the conversation and workplace problems are resolved. If you are not privy to the party, you miss key decisions or future opportunities. Many leaders show preference to employees they engage with outside of work and though they may justify social groupings as team building or reward for hard work, leaders must be mindful of "us and them cultures".

Like it or not, there are differences between feminine and masculine cultures (54) and masculinity in the workplace can also differ by level (55). For top management, it is associated with aggression and competition. In middle management, coldness and lack of emotion is a common trait. On the shop floor, machismo, seen in overtly sexual jokes and reducing women to objects, can be seen. The link between all these manifestations is power, masculine autonomy and independence (55). These characteristics are in contrast with more feminine aspects of collaboration and sense of community.

In an article titled, "I'm a female leader working in a boy's club. This is what it's like", a CEO described her experiences (56):
- Male senior management believe their job title should buy them the respect they require
- Collaboration is not on the agenda
- Referring to senior women as "love" or "girls"
- Messages with kisses
- Inappropriate jokes
- Kept at arm's length, not where the important decisions are made

She states, "the reality of a boys club is that it is allowed to exist because men and male leaders enable it to exist. All the behaviours I have described above become part of the culture of an organization.....I call out behaviours, I demand collaboration and I have the strong challenging conversations. As a result, I have been labelled the person who is hard to get along with" (56).

"SURROUND YOURSELF WITH PEOPLE WHO ARE GOING TO LIFT YOU HIGHER."

(Oprah Winfrey, media proprietor, talk show host, actress, producer, philanthropist)

So, what is a viable option? **It is for women to create their own networks** – see chapter 8 for more details. These do not need to become "girl's clubs". However, by leveraging emotional and communication skills, women are often far better networkers. Furthermore, many men and woman share beliefs and values in diversity, so enlisting the right members of management or executive teams can provide women with the more favourable professional opportunities. This may be a very deliberate action, and feel a little forced or artificial, yet men's clubs don't exist by accident either (12). Female employees are just as deserving of mentorship, sponsorship, and opportunity as their male counterparts. It is vital to create mechanisms and support networks that can provide these too!

WHAT ARE THE CORPORATE POLITICS WOMEN WANT TO AVOID?

The second aspect of corporate culture and the workplace is built around the assumption of a nuclear family with a working father and a stay-at-home mother, and one women also prefer to avoid, politics. Corporate politics is the behaviour in human interactions involving power and authority. As women prefer to pour energy into making a difference and working with close colleagues, they will often stay put in lower-level jobs and not trade what they enjoy for politics higher up which can be seen as:
• Manipulative activities
• Promotion of the undeserving
• Waste of time
• Impeding productivity
• Poor business focus

In her book, "The Politics of Promotion: How High Achieving Women Get Ahead and Stay Ahead" (57), Bonnie Marcus interviewed many women on the topic of office politics. The women described politics as dirty, manipulative, and evil. They expressed anger, frustration, and betrayal when people who spent more time schmoozing than working, would rise through the ranks faster than they did. Yet, they also viewed politics as a waste of time and were hesitant to engage in any way. This is often due to the perception that the desire for power drives noise yet impedes productivity. Highly political organizations can become unfocused, bogged down in bureaucracy, lack decision making and see people paying lip service to leaders, yet have no real commitment to implementing change.

From an organizational perspective, solutions here must be centred around solid management principles of aligned goals, empowerment and accountability and defining and ensuring acceptable behaviours for team success.

Although engaging in power games is not rewarding, women would benefit from navigating around the men's club and developing skills associated with being **more politically**

savvy. This can include improved organizational awareness related to the internal power and influence structure, for example how senior level roles are filled. Nurturing important relationships is also important and does not compromise personal integrity.

WHAT WOMEN VALUE IN THE WORKPLACE

Many studies from the last 20 years have shown that men and women value the same aspects of work but ranked them differently (58, 59, 60). Men value pay and benefits, as well as power, authority and status, significantly more than women. Women value relationships, recognition and respect, communication, fairness and equity, teams and collaboration, family and home balance. Interestingly, men do not tend to be especially aware of the factors that women value and women tend to overestimate how much men value money, status and power.

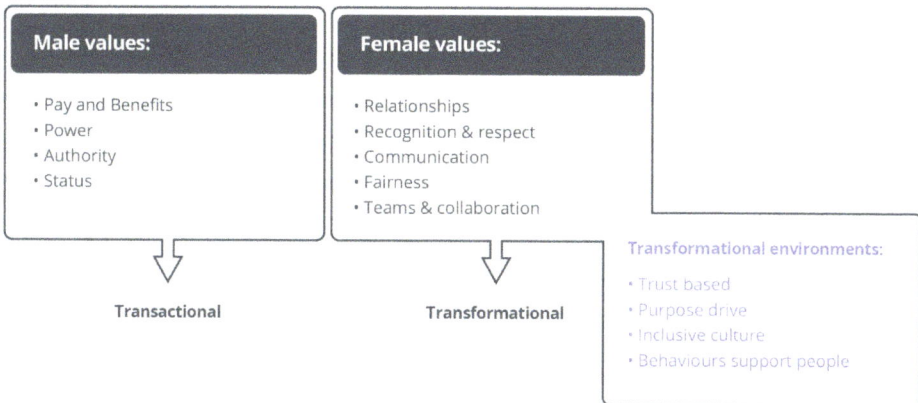

Male values:	Female values:
• Pay and Benefits	• Relationships
• Power	• Recognition & respect
• Authority	• Communication
• Status	• Fairness
	• Teams & collaboration

Transactional   Transformational

Transformational environments:
• Trust based
• Purpose drive
• Inclusive culture
• Behaviours support people

Figure 7: Top male and female values (5)

The male values seen above could be considered more transactional, and the female described as more transformational. **Transactional** is a style of leadership (61, 62) that focuses on achieving results and goals by offering transactions: Employees receive rewards for good performance, and they are punished by disciplinary actions in the case of poor performance. There is also strong association with hierarchy and task orientation. This creates an environment focused on short term task delivery and is not inspirational or ideal long term in today's complex world of constant change.

A **transformational environment** (5) is associated with **transformational leadership** and when applying this approach, managers truly act as leaders (61, 62). They actively transform their employees to a higher level of performance. It is based around trust and individuals. Focused on organizational success, employees are actively included in business purpose, decisions and outcomes. Employee development is high on the agenda and this results in employees willing to go the extra mile for business success. Understanding values suggests that women may prefer working in companies with cultures associated with transformational values.

A recent white paper by the Centre for Creative Leadership also highlights that women seek meaningful work that connects purpose and work/life balance (63). The number one reason women stay in their current role is that it fits well with other areas of their life. Women remain in companies when they enjoy the work they do and believe it provides opportunity to make a difference (purpose or calling). Women also want genuine leadership opportunities in which they are supported to achieve, not glass cliff positions with high stakes and high likelihood of failure.

This **emphasis on purpose and values** suggests that women not only favour transformational environments, but women will also choose to leave companies that fail to share such values and avoid stepping up into levels within companies where behaviours are perceived to contradict such beliefs.

CREATING A TRANSFORMATIONAL ENVIRONMENT

Once a company commits to a transformational, inclusive and diverse culture this must be defined within the corporate vision and values, implemented through strategies, policies and procedures and embedded in all behaviours. Considering the elements that make up culture, a company can then analyze and decide if current symbols, values and behaviours help to deliver company vision or hinder it.

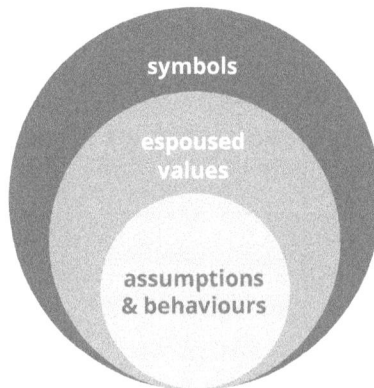

Figure 8: Changing corporate culture needs actions at 3 levels (54)

As mentioned, every business has **symbols**, from who has a corner or separate office, to the daily dress code, or who can fly business class. Symbols can extend to branding, logos and pictures on the walls. In a business committed to women in leadership and diversity overall, these visible signs must include female role models in executive positions, women presenting in company meetings and recognition for desired behaviours.

Supported **values** are seen in HR policies for fair and transparent promotions, employee development and work/life balance. The organizational structure and formal teams must include diversity, but as there are other power structures in an organization, leaders must also be cognitive here and manage this. For example, some people or groups have significant decision-making powers due to formal structures such as management teams, or they can be informal – perhaps a strong trade union able to derail or sanction decisions. As every organization also has controls (the systems for setting and maintaining standards for finance and quality), these too can be changed. Some organizations have strict standards – office time, use of emails etc. And some are looser. They can be used to steer the organization towards desired behaviours and outcomes and also used to overcome politics and bureaucracy.

Rituals and routines cover the patterns of **systematic behaviour or assumptions** that are seen as normal. These rituals can be positive – supporting colleagues, sponsoring women, collaborative team work etc. But they can be negative such as bullying, sexism, the men's club etc that need to be stamped out!

Culture can also be changed from within. Overcoming office politics can be impacted by individuals wanting to contribute, by praising others, encouraging teamwork and being empathetic to co-workers. People who make an effort to change the culture to one of kindness and honesty can create a better environment for everyone.

There are excellent examples of cultures to emulate and while there are plenty of companies doing diversity right, these ones really stand out as places women want to be part of (64):

L'ORÉAL	Strong board.

L'Oreal, the multinational cosmetics company is present in 130 countries and focuses on multiculturalism in the workplace. Not only that, 69% of its workforce are women, 53% of key positions are held by women and 8 of 15 board members are also women (company statistics 2019)

Alibaba.com	**Strong values.**

Alibaba Group, the world's biggest e-commerce company claims its secret is "women's perseverance and attention to detail". One third of the founders and executives are women. The company also achieves high employee engagement with values including teamwork, integrity, passion and commitment (Alibaba.com)

Lenovo	**Strong culture.**

Lenovo, the world's largest PC vendor, has built its success on a strong foundation of diversity and inclusion. They define their own culture as "a company where all add value, and where all belong." And why is this important? In the words of Yolanda Conyers, the company's chief diversity officer, "serving a global customer base requires more than out-of-the-box thinking, because it's not just one box. It's a million different boxes. It takes every dimension of our diversity, all our diverse mindsets, skills, and cultural backgrounds, to deliver such a wide array of technology" (64).

FINDING PURPOSE ALIGNED WITH VALUES

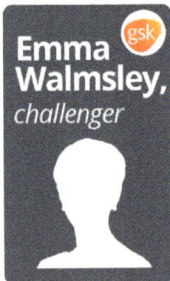

Emma Walmsley, *challenger*

In 2017, Emma Walmsley was appointed new CEO of GSK, the first woman to head up a major global pharmaceutical company. In 2018 she was awarded Britain's Most Admired Leader by journal Management Today (22).

Before GSK, she was General Manager for Garnier/ Maybelline at L'Oréal. Her success as a world-class leader is attributed to a winning combination of (66): IQ, technical experience from a variety of international marketing and management roles, commercial savviness and EQ (Emotional Quotient, a measure of emotional intelligence), enabling her to engage and motivate others to be the very best that they can be.

On gender equality in modern business, Emma Walmsley has said "you cannot be a modern employer in an industry that should be future facing and modernizing without being very demanding on this topic." She believes companies "should be much more proactive about sponsoring and supporting all types of diversity to get to the senior leadership positions". As such, she recognizes her own "responsibility as a leader, as a role model". She also declares, "I love working for a company whose purpose I believe in" (67). Her clear belief in the type of company she wants to be in also mirrors research on what women value in the workplace.

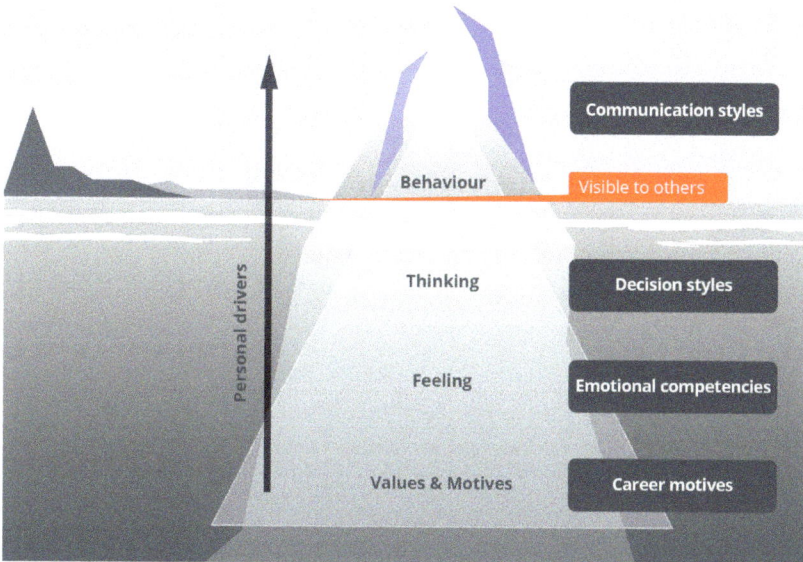

Figure 9: How our values and motives drive what we like to do (5)

Personal values are one's own principles of behaviour or our judgement of what is important in life. Motives are what make us tick. Both of these define the activities people like to do and how they invest their time and energy. They also drive feelings, thinking and behaviours.

Values are even more important to understand for leaders as authentic leadership and influence comes from leaders knowing their own values and motives. In other words, for a leader to behave authentically to lead others, seeing these connections and staying true to personal values is critical. Especially in difficult times, disruptive change, restructuring and other examples of uncertainty, leaders are often required to deliver tough messages, reshape teams and even close business areas. The decision point is not whether to act or when, it is how a leader approaches the task and handles the individuals. This is when trust, respect and integrity count.

Not only do individuals have values, but also companies have values as part of corporate culture and together with vision, mission and strategies, they form the **identity of the company**. Finding alignment of personal and company values is motivating and essential.

As a leader, knowing the company story, focusing on goals and key projects, and believing in the company journey is a key part of the role. As a leader, it is therefore important to consider if personal values and motives are aligned with the company's. Many would choose not to work for an oil company if the company exploited natural resources ruthlessly. Many may not wish to work for a hire and fire type organization that did not believe in its people. Many women choose not to work in an organization that does not value collaboration and community. So, as a leader, you have to ask yourself: Does this company behave in a way you are comfortable with?

WHY WORK FOR A PARTICULAR ORGANIZATION?

Company identify is not only important for employees for meaning and direction, identity is also crucial for people's decisions to join a specific company. In summary (63), women join companies for:
• Purpose
• Personal career development
• Atmosphere

Women remain in companies for:
• Work / life balance
• Enjoyment of the work and people
• Continued purpose
• Genuine leadership opportunities in which they are supported to achieve

This emphasis on purpose and values again suggests that women not only favour transformational environments, but women will also choose to leave companies that fail to share such values and avoid stepping up into levels within companies where behaviours are perceived to contradict such beliefs.

For many women, if the environment in which they work plays a huge part in their success, what are the options?
• Seek out best places, because they do exist?
• Leave specific jobs for success and happiness elsewhere?
• Stay put in jobs where there is a sense of meaning and pursue greater satisfaction across other parts of life?
• Or pour energy into making a difference?

Whatever route women take, it is clear that belief is required in whatever we are doing. For any woman in a leadership role, you must also be aligned with organizational values and act as a role model for such values, to create a context and meaning for those around you.

And it is true, that for women in leadership, the challenge of being a great leader, as well as pushing boundaries and breaking down barriers can be immense.

KEY LEARNING POINTS ON CULTURAL BARRIERS

- Corporate culture is not written down, but it involves beliefs and social behaviours of groups of people. It shapes how things are done and how employees experience the workplace

- The Men's Club or Boy's Club is associated with group activities unrelated to everyone's defined jobs and used to bestow social legitimacy, solidarity and group recognition. These clubs depend on exclusivity for their power and women are rarely admitted. During these social engagements, work talk is included in the conversation, workplace problems are resolved, and new job opportunities and suitable candidates discussed. Exclusion from the "club" can mean exclusion from workplace success

- Corporate politics is the behaviour in human interactions involving power and authority. It is one few women engage in as it can be seen as manipulative, giving promotions to the undeserving and a waste of time causing poor productivity and poor business focus

- Women have different values at work and tend to value relationships, recognition and respect, communication, fairness and equity, teams and collaboration, family and home balance

- Women's emphasis on purpose and values suggests women favour transformational environments, women will choose to leave companies that fail to share such values and avoid stepping up into levels within companies where behaviours are perceived to contradict such beliefs

- Corporate culture can be changed from within but finding alignment of personal and company values is motivating and essential

Chapter Five

HOW TO CONNECT MEN AND WOMEN FOR BETTER RESULTS

Penguins are pragmatic in teams

Research on gender and collaboration has shown that for men, being a good team player is all about knowing your position and playing it well (70). Men have also been shown to be better than women at focusing on priorities, even allocating protected time to getting their things done. These practical approaches to teamwork are important to note since women have a tendency to take on more collaborative burden in teams due to belief that being a good team player means caring for the collective, to the point of stepping in to fill gaps left by others and giving away personal time if someone else needs us.

Why do we need to know this? Well, in today's world, working in teams is everywhere and women must know how to work well in teams with men. They are not the enemy; they just work differently, and remember, different is good.

THE IMPORTANCE OF TEAMWORK

Teamwork is the collaborative effort of a group of people to achieve a common goal or to complete a task in the most effective and efficient way (4). Teamwork requires significant planning, structure and understanding to achieve active participant and effect results. It is also required more and more in today's workplace with project teams and matrix organizations (5) and with the rise of virtual teams and remote working, this is only set to continue. It is also our reality that teams need to be mixed. As said in chapter one, homogeneous teams are extremely limiting, and diverse teams deliver the best results! At extremes, men-only teams can demonstrate high risk-taking, which is tempered when women are included (68). Women-only teams have been known to be bitchy... On the other hand, teams with men and women make better decisions. Simply put, we are better together. So, how do we ensure we connect well with men and don't see "men" as the enemy? What can we learn and apply to be more pragmatic in teams and ensure men and women cooperate and collaborate well?

Let's consider the **traits of high-performing teams** to be clear on what we are aiming for, then we will look at how to achieve this. So, for teams to function well over time they need the following (69):
• diverse talents for expertise and insights
• shared purpose and direction
• motivating goals
• all members understanding their roles
• all members committed to joint success
• willingness to support and trust one another
• authority for decision making
• good communication in all directions

The best advice I ever received... Sabine Decker
Build a team around you that challenge you, balance your own weakness and who have full trust in each other.

HOW TO INTEGRATE MEN AND WOMEN

Do you remember the old team building phases of forming, storming, norming and performing? Well, there is still some truth to this cycle. To form a team, not matter the make-up, active steps have to be taken. Trust does not arise on its own and goals are never achieved if they are not aligned. Diversity is not valued if the value of diversity is not shared and embedded across the organization. The key factor for forming a successful team is **transparency** (70) because transparency helps you to be clear about your intentions and being transparent means working in a way that is honest and open to others.

> "A lack of transparency results in distrust and a deep sense of insecurity" (71)

Transparency when instigating a new project team for example, must include the following aspects at the team kick-off:

- Clear team / project goals – Goals should always be SMART (specific, measurable, aligned with business needs, realistic and timed). Broader definition of the purpose, scope and key milestones can also add weight and clarity.
- Who does what – especially important is to introduce people, allow people to share information about their areas of expertise and distribute personal contact information. If everyone knows who's doing what, it reduces ambiguity and it is easier for people to hold one another accountable.
- Defined expectations for team working methods and reporting – this will include how work is documented, actions agreed, decisions made, and next steps followed up. It can also include rules of conduct if necessary if there has been limited interaction in the past, new cultural elements or diversity topics to be highlighted.

To truly integrate diversity of all types, **an inclusive team has to be based on trust.** Trust is the precursor to engagement with tasks, projects or teams. Only once people are engaged is it possible for them to move further and be fully committed to achieve best outcomes with others (4). When there is genuine trust between people, it means allowing vulnerability, to speak openly about a mistake for example, because the expectation is that the other person will react in a positive way. The goal of trust is therefore to create an environment of openness and honesty, allowing people to show their weaknesses as well as strengths, without fear of recrimination or abuse. Whether you are a team leader or a team player, you have to choose to trust others. When we trust someone, we have confidence in them and in their honesty and integrity. We believe that they will do the things they say they will. We recognize their abilities and strengths, and we place our faith in them. To generate trust, you need to listen empathetically, be authentic and act according to what you say. Shared values, manners and respect for all are fundamental. In general, trust is what individuals reflect back. Hence it starts by being open and transparent; being dependable, consistent, and reliable; and taking responsibility when things don't work out quite as planned.

Trust is also a principle of effective management (72). Especially in the virtual world where managers cannot see their employees, and team members don't always know each other well, increasing levels of trust are required, not increasing levels of control! Trust is the reason why managers and teams can be successful even when they make mistakes. Conflicts or difficulties can be solved, based on trusting relationships. This is because trust is fostered through great communication, positive influence and working in a psychologically safe environment in which all can thrive (4). If you wish to learn more about the secret of trust and how you can develop your personal communication and influence, we recommend our book "Connecting and Influencing: A Leader's Guide to Genuine Communication" (4).

"TO BUILD TRUST, TELL THE TRUTH"

(Simon Sinek, Author and inspirational speaker)

HOW TO LEVERAGE CONTRIBUTIONS FROM ALL SIDES

For most of us, work has a broader meaning. It is not a simple task, we don't just do it for the money. For most, work is about fulfilment, engaging our minds and nourishing our souls. The challenge comes when it is not fun, it is not engaging or there are issues related to unfairness, politics etc. In these situations, if we are not careful, we can lose direction. Work can become more about just ticking the box and less about the purpose or outcomes. It can also be more difficult then to work with other people and work effectively in teams. So how do we keep teams focused? It is all about focus...

First and foremost, **focus on results and contribution** (72). Having a results orientation refers to having clear objectives or goals and making sure that this is what everyone cares about. This is based on the principal motivation coming from common direction. It occurs from setting goals which allow individual initiative and responsibility, promote teamwork and aligns the goals of all individuals with the business interests. In whatever context you are in, be it in a team or leading a team, ask yourself are the expected results clear? It is not about control when you focus on whether people achieve the agreed results. Control or micro-management happens when you hone in on how or what people do. Focus on results provides a framework for everyone, helping them to orientate, showing them where to go and where priorities lie. This orientation defines expectations and defines the individual's contributions to the overall company success. It is good thing! Furthermore, focusing on contributing to the whole also allows you to explain what others are working on. It can be compared to an orchestra where every musician is a specialist in their area, yet each musician has to play together for the overall effect. Thinking back to our learning from penguins, men are much better at focusing on delivering their part, allocating the time to do so and women need to apply this approach more. How? Focus on the right things!

It is another key principle of management to **concentrate on a few things** instead of trying to complete everything (72). Yes, this is challenging in a complex world with hundreds of different tasks and yes this may be more challenging for women who feel the need to support the wider team more, yet when we are not able to bundle our concentration and energy to do excellent work we are inefficient. Hence concentration is the key to achieving results as it helps avoid wasting energy and time. The necessary skills here include time management, prioritization, and delegation. It allows for the team tasks and projects to be organized and requires you to be organized in your personal work methods, such as ensuring undisturbed working time.

Lastly, to ensure all team members can contribute their best and contribute to results, the final focus area is the **focus on individual strengths** (72). Sadly, human nature has a tendency to focus on what is lacking yet better motivation and productivity occur when we understand differences and position people so they use more of who they are and what their strengths are, in other words, their talents. Cultivating and using strengths at work enables success and enhances employee well-being! It needs encouraging though and should be an active decision when integrating men and women in teams. As Albert Einstein famously said, "... if you judge a fish by its ability to climb a tree, it will live its whole life believing that it is stupid". Let's not propagate such negative thinking.

> "EXCITEMENT COMES FROM THE ACHIEVEMENT.
> FULFILMENT COMES FROM THE JOURNEY
> THAT GOT YOU THERE"
> (Simon Sinek, Author and inspirational speaker)

HOW TO REDUCE GROUPTHINK

Positive thinking is part of good teamwork and collaboration. Thinking is also key to diverse team success, but as mentioned, groupthink can be a serious derailer of effective teamwork. Groupthink is the exaggerated desire for agreement and harmony that endangers realistic assessments and decision-making (14). Overcoming this is essential for a productive, creative and critical thinking atmosphere. It starts from a team being heterogeneous but also requires steering. To involve all people in finding new and better ways, teams and or leaders needs to **ensure all voices are heard**, not just the loudest ones, and especially women who may show the tendency not to speak up or ask for what they need. Examples of how to do this include (4):

- Actively seeking ways to involve everyone in an active process to seek out different views
- Asking each member to contribute separately, even if it means in writing beforehand
- Specifically, directing questions at any quieter team members to avoid loss of the "lonely genius"
- Asking for expert inputs to collect facts, not unsubstantiated opinions
- Giving people time to formulate ideas
- Ignoring convention and boundaries when gathering other insights and perspectives
- Being seen to be open to contributions from all sides by listening and integrating points
- Challenging given statements and norms to question the status quo
- Seeking options and alternative solutions, not problems or limitations
- Always being aware that, as a leader, if you state your viewpoint first, this will always limit new ideas from surfacing as some people are often reluctant to contradict the leader

As a leader, balance is always required in group settings: Too little involvement can be inefficient and too much direction stifles the creativity of others. In group settings, stimulating group interactions is all about the mindset to collaborate, the willingness to speak up, get involved and actively contributing throughout the entire work process, but often in different personal roles (4).

LACK OF INVOLVEMENT	BALANCED ENGAGEMENT	TAKING OVER
Issues	Personal role	Issues
• Can appear arrogant or disinterested (unsetting for others)	• To guide towards outcome (ask questions)	• "My way" (demotivating for others)
• Let meetings run over time with no outcomes (inefficient)	• To provide own expertise (share knowledge or skills)	• No new ideas (limits innovation)
	• To facilitate (provide framework or structure)	• No collective problem solving (no buy-in)

Figure 10: Finding balanced engagement for effective meetings

Guiding meetings is seeking active participation to engage and include all the group, including quieter members by actively asking for their opinion, asking specific questions, summarizing points, following up on inputs and enabling the group to reach outcomes such as decisions or actions plans.

Contributing content in meetings seeks to influence the group based on valuable input such as expertise and requires clear messages that are accepted by the group. To be listened to, it is about a message that inspires others, based on a shared vision or showing what's in it for them, and using language all will understand. It is essential to explain reasoning or thinking to get buy-in and checking that others are in agreement, never assume!

Structuring meetings or facilitating meetings can be advantageous to manage a larger group meeting to ensure that the objectives are met effectively, with good participation and buy-in from everyone who is involved. Taking such a formal approach works when you are objective, so not necessarily involved in the topic, and key is enabling the meeting to flow from group ideas, to solutions, through to decisions. Structure can include:

- Setting the scene – welcoming, introducing people, breaking the ice, reviewing objectives and reviewing the agenda
- Controlling flow – following a model to distil data to knowledge, wisdom and outcomes
- Blending participation – balancing inputs from set speaker time to discussion time or use of breakout groups and exercises. Using questioning to augment ideas and include everyone
- Reviewing inputs, reframing, and summarizing
- Pausing and reflecting – giving individual thinking time and not coercing others
- Closing – documenting decisions, tasks and next steps

What is critical to understand when you want to get the most out of meetings is that compared to women, men tend to talk more and make more suggestions, while women are interrupted more, given less credit for their ideas, and have less overall influence (73). Tips to overcome this include encouraging women to sit in the front at meetings, interjecting when a female colleague is interrupted and openly asking women to contribute to the conversation. Also, be aware of "stolen ideas" and look for opportunities to acknowledge the women who first proposed them. These steps enhance full participation in meetings so you can tap everyone's skills and expertise and improve team outcomes.

"IF EVERYONE IS MOVING FORWARD TOGETHER, THEN SUCCESS TAKES CARE OF ITSELF"

(Henry Ford, Founder of the Ford Motor Company)

HOW TO BUILD SPIRIT IN VIRTUAL SCENARIOS OR ACROSS REMOTE TEAMS

The meeting is a key management tool and meetings serve functions (74) such as defining a group or team, revising and updating what is known by the group, agreeing goals and understanding individual contributions, decision making and enabling the leader to shape the way the group succeeds. In more collaborative cultures, meetings may be seen to escalate to the point of inefficiency due to too many participants and few outcomes, however, especially in the world of more virtual working, meetings are critical to ensure distance does not become an issue.

Firstly, let's just review the **common elements of successful meetings** (4):
• A clear goal or objective for the meeting
• Reason for who is present
• Documentation, either for preparation or follow up
• An agenda, structure and rules, including who is responsible for leading the meeting
• An outcome and actions

Whether a meeting is face-to-face or online, the elements above apply. However, if we consider team meetings and integration in the virtual world, we do need to understand the psychology of teams and why, in this world of "zoom", do many people feel "zoomed out". In the physical world it is the problem of poor planning and preparation that causes meeting fatigue – no agenda, off topic distractions, lack of preparation, no decisions or outcomes.... In the online world, the main frustraters are technical issues followed by the **emotional challenges of isolation** and the fatigue caused by 24/7 pressure. For the technical challenges such as poor sound or visual quality, background noise, connection cut-offs etc, you simply need to get familiar with how to fix them or how to help others fix them at their end! To avoid the emotional challenges and connect better with remote colleagues, you need to understand the new issues and how to overcome them. Distance can hinder relationships with the boss and other colleagues. It will also diminish team spirit. Feeling isolated can also occur due to limited interactions, no feedback, no chat, not knowing who to ask for input or due to reluctance to use technology required for good virtual communication and collaboration.

Ultimately, what we are looking to maintain, despite distance or being physically present, is the sense of **purpose and connectedness to something bigger than ourselves**. Being part of a team, be it remotely, helps us focus on collective outcomes (results and contributions), as well as human wellbeing in our complex world. A key success factor is to create **team spirit** across remote teams. Team spirit is the feeling of pride and loyalty that exists among the members of a team and that makes them want their team to do well or to be the best. As footballer Thomas Muller said, "team spirit is paramount – each of our own egos has to take a back seat...".

In the virtual workplace, creating team spirit can be more difficult yet the bond and togetherness from "water cooler chat" is possible in the virtual business world. The 2 billion Facebook users is testament to the social abilities of humans to connect across the world when there is shared interest to do so. It has to start from the manager actively engaging the team, ensuring the team identifies with organizational or business values and goals. Team setup, structure and formal ways of working also begin to establish collaborative work and shared responsibility. But you also need to decide on how you want the team to behave and then role model the behaviour too. If you don't actively decide and act on "culture", it will create itself anyway and maybe not the way you would prefer. **Culture** is the glue of identity and belonging for the team and seen in actions and behaviours. Sometimes even tiny things can have a huge impact; just think back to the negative corporate cultures we looked at in chapter 4! So, how can you inspire others and create a **cohesive and inclusive team spirit** remotely?

Here are some tips (75):
1. Technology counts - Knowing it is one thing but actively using it remotely and with finesse is another thing. Everyone needs to be onboard with using all the tools possible to connect.
2. The mindset for virtual collaboration – This includes time and willingness to integrate everyone and actively include and integrate all team members. This is true not only for meetings to inform but also taking time with people one-to-one.
3. There is no "i" in team – No one is in this alone. Ask the team for inputs as asking questions stimulates our brains to find solutions and the more brains, the more ideas. Also, encourage others take initiative and get involved.
4. Never assume - When you have vision and goals, talk about them a lot. Talk about your values, how you work, how to find information. It is so easy to forget what is going on when you are miles apart so keep up the conversations.
5. Spirit and culture come from rituals - Establish new rituals together. These can be as simple as how meetings are opened, how chat apps are used or even having crazy virtual backgrounds.
6. It is still all about team building – This comes from the social, not only the work interactions. Do things together as a virtual team – huddles, shared coffee breaks and even after work beers are surprisingly nice when done via video chat!
7. Celebrate team successes - One of the main reasons people leave their jobs is that they don't feel appreciated. When a manager takes time to demonstrate gratitude and appreciation for team and individual accomplishments it can motivate, engage, and reinforce positive behaviours and outcomes. It is also important to create a positive culture where team feedback is exchanged, so use the online meeting to share praise and spark a sense of joy.

"INCLUSION IS NOT SIMPLY ABOUT PROXIMITY.
IT IS ABOUT INTENTIONALLY PLANNING
FOR THE SUCCESS OF ALL..."

(Tim Villegas, Author)

WORKING IN TEAMS IS A COMPETENCY REQUIRED BY ALL WORKERS

Throughout this book we are aiming to highlight the abilities and competencies women need to develop to be successful in leadership. The next 4 chapters in particular are targeting individual development and impact. Here we wish to summarize what working in inclusive teams means as a competency as this is required by all workers, men and women alike and is vital to shape success at all levels, across all geographies and integrating all forms of diversity. It is also not always about being friends with others but acting with professionalism at all times.

Working in teams means successfully working with others to achieve common goals. It includes being able to build constructive working relationships with managers, co-workers, customers and partners, and such relationships are characterized by a high level of acceptance, trust, cooperation and mutual respect. Behaviours associated with teamwork are:

• Relating to everyone in an open, honest and respectful manner.
• Being considerate of others, regardless of gender, race, ethnicity, age, sexual orientation, social background, religion, education or status: Actively involving all others where appropriate and encouraging cooperation across teams or groups.
• Respecting the opinion of others, empathizing with other's needs, listening to their perspectives and supporting other ideas or inputs.
• Liaising with others concerning the completion of tasks, hence achieving common goals.
• Sharing information, contributing ideas or solutions, and meeting agreed deadlines.
• Willing to speak up and address issues that hinder progress or productivity in a non-judgemental or threatening manner.
• Constructively working with people of different departments, cultures and across geographical distances.
• Being accountable for team results.

KEY LEARNING POINTS ON CONNECTEDNESS IN DIVERSE TEAMS

- Connectedness is about connecting with and integrating others and the business

- It is choosing to include others at all times

- Collaborative teamwork is a critical element for success today

- Diverse teams are more successful than similar teams as they share wider perspectives, challenge thinking, consider new ideas and solutions, and make better decisions

- Integrating men and women in teams also gives better balance

- Mixed teams thrive when there is transparency on goals, roles and expectations

- Trust across a team is the precursor for task engagement and commitment to achieving joint success

- Highly effective and inclusive teams focus on results, contributions, priorities and people strengths

- Team leaders need to actively steer teams to shape culture, run effective meetings and avoid groupthink

- Team spirit, the feeling of pride and loyalty that makes people want their team to do well or to be the best, can be achieved even for virtual teams when effort and time is invested to create a bond of shared purpose and connectedness

- It is ultimately about doing your job with full professionalism

Chapter Six

MINDSET AND ATTITUDE ARE KEY FOR SELF-BELIEF

How penguins attribute
success

In a senior management meeting we attended, there were prizes awarded for special achievement. What was interesting was the different reactions of male and female managers to the rewards bestowed. The first male manager received $2000, and duly thanked everyone for appreciating his work. Second and third male managers received their awards, and the same procedure. Then a female manager received a reward and firstly thanked her team and recognized that she would not have achieved the results or award without them. She then went on to say the financial reward would not be for herself but would be shared with the team.

So, what was going on? What the penguins demonstrated was an underlying principle of how men and women relate to success and failure differently. What this theory shows (76) is that success or failure is either attributed to internal factors (such as competence or effort) or external factors, related to the situation which are either stable or variable. Now if you transfer the theoretical model to the example, it is obvious that the men in the example showed a tendency to attribute success internally – the success was directly linked to themselves and their competence or efforts. Whereas the female manager immediately attributed it externally, in this case to the team effort and the team competence.

SHOWING SUCCESS

Differences in attribution once again highlight that women are often silent about their individual successes and talk much more about the team and other external factors which helped. Men on the contrary usually communicate their individual successes a lot more openly and broadly. In the context of working at a senior management level, having confidence in our abilities and speaking up about them is definitely something that we as women need to do more of! This is where we will start as we explore how to succeed as a woman in leadership by shifting the scales in our favour.

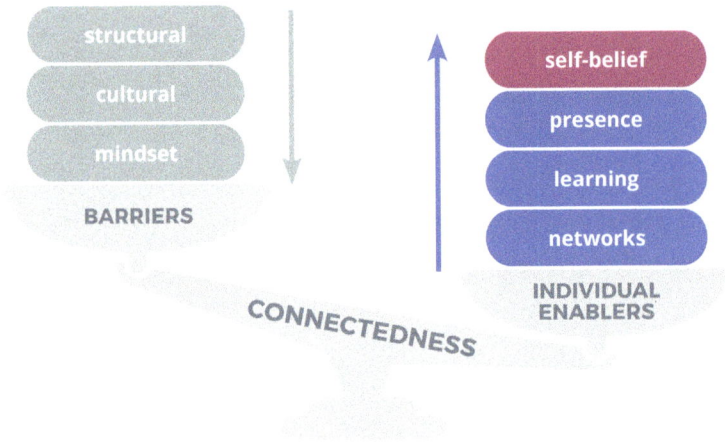

Figure 11: Shifting the scales for individual success starts with self-belief

Self-belief starts with our **mindset and attitude**, which impacts the way we think about ourselves and how we behave (3). As said, our individual mindset is all about the assumptions, methods, or notions we hold. In other words, our attitude. As a rule, attitude is a settled way of feeling or thinking about something or someone, yet we can make a choice to change how we react to situations or people. We can, with effort, change our habitual reactions, break our bad habits!

THE LEADERSHIP CHALLENGE

In our global and digitalized world with constant disruptive change, cultural differences and dealing with individuals with differing needs and interests, leaders are faced with immense challenges daily. To reflect this outside world, we expect leaders to adapt and be relevant at all times. This means leaders need to be stable yet flexible, coherent yet embracing complexity. For women, we are also expected to deliver consistently higher performance yet are offered little support by way of mentorship. Leaders are also expected to be role models, yet women have few role models at CEO level. This near impossible tight rope or balancing act requires well developed leadership skills and competencies, as well as mental and emotional maturity and stability.

FIRST IMPRESSIONS

As we looked at in chapter 1, a significant challenge for women is how we are judged and the biases that we face. As the saying goes "first impressions count" and impressions individuals give to others greatly influence how they are viewed and treated at work. You only have seven seconds to make a good first impression (77) because humans are programmed to make quick judgements. If you want to be taken seriously as a leader you have to dress the part, act the part and behave consistently, in other words how people expect managers to behave. It is not conforming per se, it is visible professionalism to building respect and trust (5). We will explore looking the part in chapter 6. Here we begin with how to act the part, and this starts with understanding how you feel, think and behave.

"WHETHER YOU THINK YOU CAN OR YOU THINK YOU CAN'T, YOU'RE RIGHT."
(Henry Ford, Founder of the Ford Motor Company)

What is critical for any leader is enjoying what we do and working in an environment that makes us happy. When we discussed values, we referred to understanding what make us tick (see figure 9). To really understand ourselves, we also need to understand how "what" we express to others, so our behaviours and our actions, is driven by how we feel and think.

HOW WE ENSURE WE PROJECT
THE BEST BEHAVIOURS OR ACTIONS

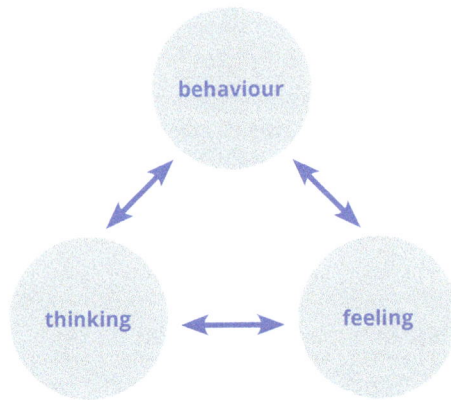

Figure 12: The powerful link between feeling, thinking and behaviour

Our **behaviour** in business is not only important as it is how we judged, but also because our actions can directly impact other workers and team members. Our visible behaviours, such as what we say or do, can be seen in our communication style and this impacts how successful we are when we interact with others.

Thinking is all about how we plan, solve problems and make decisions and this impacts how successfully we deliver results.

In a business context, when we consider feelings, what we are referring to are **emotional competencies** and emotional intelligence. How we deal with our own and others' feelings impacts how successfully we manage our own emotions, anticipate reactions of others and understand how to be effective in social or stressful situations. The biggest challenge is the power of unchecked emotions, especially under stress. The moment you lose emotional control, you lose the ability for good decision making, effective communication and therefore positive influence (4). Strong emotional intelligence is essential for leaders (78) and more important than IQ (79). Remember the good news, "women outperform men in 11 of 12 key emotional intelligence competencies crucial for effective leadership" (7). Specifically, this research found that women demonstrated the following emotional competencies better than men, so ask yourself how you would rate yourself of them too:

- **Self-awareness** – having a conscious knowledge of yourself, including the ability to form an accurate self-concept and understand the impact you have on others

- **Empathy** – the ability to understand others' strong and weak points, as well as their motives
- **Coaching and mentoring** – skills and mindset to actively support the development of others
- **Inspiration** – mentally stimulating others to do or feel something
- **Influence** – the power to cause someone to change a behaviour, belief, or opinion, based on motivation and common vision
- **Conflict management** – ability to limit the negative aspects of serious disagreement between others to enhance group outcomes
- **Organizational awareness** – understanding all aspects of the organization including workings, structure and culture, to effect plans and align actions
- **Adaptability** – willingness and capacity to adapt and modify behaviour to adjust to new conditions, situations or people
- **Teamwork** – willingness and ability to participate and contribute to the combined action of a group in an effective and efficient manner
- **Achievement orientation** – focusing on results and valuing the contributions from all parties
- **Positive outlook** – constructive thinking and an upbeat attitude, including being optimistic about situations, interactions and yourself

Emotional **self-control** was the only competency in this study in which men and women showed equal performance (7). Requirement for composure is all about remaining cool and unflustered in the face of frustrations or difficulties, appearing solid, trustworthy, consistent and able to make sound judgements.

It is in the area of **self-confidence**, having trust in oneself, that many women fall short (65, 80). Confidence however is a balance. It is projecting self-assurance and ambition and the willingness to take on work that is highly challenging, even if that may involve significant risk and/or conflict. However, when self-confidence is too high, arrogance can be the result, along-side over-estimating your own capabilities. Too low though, a person can be perceived as overly cautious and reluctant to undertake difficult assignments. Confidence is valuable as a competence because it leads to action, attention and resilience (81).

Men are not exempt from doubting themselves, yet they don't let their doubts stop them as often as women do. The female confidence challenge was also described as the "**imposter syndrome**", referring to an internal experience of believing that you are not as competent as others perceive you to be (82). Women frequently express that they don't feel they deserve their job and are "imposters" who could be found out at any moment. The difference is that as men progress, their feelings of doubt usually abate as their work and intelligence are validated over time. They're able to find role models who are like them, and rarely do others question their competence, contributions, or leadership style (83).

Women on the other hand tend to worry more about being disliked, appearing unattractive, outshining others, or grabbing too much attention (82). There may be hormonal and brain function reasons for this, however it is often the actual exclusion and stereotyping that actually makes it worse (84).

HOW TO BUILD SELF-CONFIDENCE

Confidence is a feeling or belief. It is believing in someone or something, hence self-confidence is linked to self-belief or self-trust. We experience self-confidence in two different forms (85):
- General Self-Confidence as a stable personality trait. This is our level of general self-confidence based on our beliefs and judgments about our ability to do well irrespective of the task or context. It develops early in our lives, within the contexts of our families and other social environments.
- Specific Self-Confidence is a variable state of mind reflecting our beliefs and feelings about our ability to do a specific task that we are facing at a particular point in time. Like general self-confidence, specific self-confidence is built primarily on our judgements about our performances. However, unlike general self-confidence it is a state of mind that alters in some way after almost every new experience; hence can increase when we learn to do a specific task and succeed in performing it, but when we fail, this task-specific confidence may fall.

We develop both types of self-confidence through automatic, mostly unconscious, internal dialogues whereby we make judgements about ourselves based on our experiences and others' feedback. Other actions can include (81):
- **Mindset** to enhance the way you think about yourself
  - Focus on strengths and your achievements, rather than what you don't do well. Guard carefully against negative self-talk. Never put yourself down or others will also do this.
  - Radiate optimism and general happiness as your behaviour changes your inner feelings.
  - Project warmness towards others as people are attracted to those who are perceived as "warm" and shy away from those who are perceived as "cold."
  - Be open minded to anything new, to new perspectives, new ideas and new learning

- **Mannerisms** to transmit a sense of confidence to others
  - Speak up in meetings, be an active participant.
  - Interact with many people, ask questions to engage others.
  - Initiate contact with others, don't wait for others to come to you.
  - Laugh with others over gentle banter regarding topics of mutual interest.
  - Walk briskly, convey importance.

HOW TO INCREASE YOUR EMOTIONAL INTELLIGENCE

Emotional intelligence is the understanding of and managing your own emotions and those of the people around you for greater connectedness (4). It impacts your ability to project an authentic, professional yet caring manner, portraying a style of communication most effective in any given situation, building rapport and building relationships. It is why it is so important in all aspects of life!

Have high emotional intelligence is linked to brain function and it is something that you can develop when you understand the link between feeling, thinking and acting. Emotions can have an effect on your brain before you understand what you feel and can therefore hijack rational thinking and result in poor actions (79). This is all instinct and our fight-or-flight survival instinct is still very powerful and if left unchecked can lead to poor reactions. On the other hand, those with high emotional intelligence are able to overcome this quick impulsive response and employ rational thought, to perceive, control and evaluate emotions and use this information to guide thinking and actions. This is known as emotional separation, enabling inner calm in difficult circumstances and retention of the ability to think rationally and use relevant competencies in order to take high quality decisions and then act or communicate in the best way, even in stressful situations.

Daniel Goleman, the "father" of emotional intelligence, defined 5 elements to frame this ability towards yourself and other people (79). Here is a summary of what it is all about and ways to enhance each of the elements (4):

TIPS FOR ENHANCING EMOTIONAL INTELLIGENCE ELEMENTS FOR BETTER COMMUNICATION WITH OTHERS:			
EI ELEMENT	BENEFITS	DOS	DON'TS
Self-awareness	Realistic self-image	Admit weaknesses and mistakes. Act upon feedback.	Blame external factors for problems. Ignore how you affect other people.
Self-regulation	Able to manage stress, avoid outbursts.	Pause, think & listen before acting. Consider alternative approaches. Know your mood shifters.	Make impulsive decisions or act when feeling mad, bad or sad. Take things personally.

EI ELEMENT	BENEFITS	DOS	DON'TS
Self-movitvation	Confidence, intrisically driven, not seeking approval or recognition from others.	Find inner belief. Act with humility. Be open to changes and challenges, keep learning, set personal goals.	Demand recognition. Make winning everything. Get angry when you are not appreciated.
Social awareness (empathy)	Connecting with others, showing you care.	Observe, listen & consider others. Treat all with respect. Be generous with time, feedback & info. Follow your intuition.	Stereotype or judge others. Ignore other's input or concerns. Ignore other's feelings. Make assumptions.
Social regulation (social skills)	Connecting with others, building rapport and relationships.	Be curious, excited, open & honest. Welcome people, address with names. Improve questioning & empathetic listening. Compromise, find solutions together. Use positive body language. Praise others, let others shine.	Tell or insist on being right. Communicate only in "your way". Hide or ignore people or problems. Be distracted when talking to people. Hold grudges.

Figure 13: Enhancing emotional intelligence

PRACTICING SELF-REFLECTION

As seen above, self-awareness is the cornerstone of emotional intelligence. It is also an essential factor in staying sane (6). Self-awareness is a key starting point for developing self-belief as it means having a conscious knowledge of one's own attitudes, motives and values and how these are linked to feelings or emotions and then to actions or behaviours.

The ability for self-understanding helps form an accurate self-concept to operate effectively and for further development of emotional health, the ability to have strong sense of self is also needed. Sadly, surveys have shown many people do not show high self-awareness or self-reflection despite many teachings indicating this insight as fundamental for personal change and growth.

"HE WHO KNOWS OTHERS IS WISE; HE WHO KNOWS HIMSELF IS ENLIGHTENED."

(Lao Tzu, ancient Chinese philosopher and writer)

Self-reflection is the exercise on introspection, such as reviewing your own strengths and development areas, acknowledging your achievements and limitations, considering your role in situations, showing willingness to seek feedback and to learn more. Through self-reflection or observation, it makes self-responsibility possible, and it is essential for adult-based learning (5). If we never reflect, think about what went wrong and how we can be better, we keep on making the same old mistakes...

To dos:
- Be clear on your personal **strengths to leverage** at work and accept weaknesses or imperfections and work on them. Write lists and define personal action plans.
- Be brave and **speak up about your achievements.** What are you really proud of?
- **Accept praise** with grace. Simply say "thank you" when others give positive feedback or compliments.
- Have courage to **seek new inputs**. By actively seeking feedback from others, it is possible to understand if your self-image is the same as others' views and to learn from different perceptions and perspectives.
- **Examine your reactions to stressful situations** and avoid blaming others or becoming angry. Did you help the situation? What could you have done differently? Staying calm in difficult situations and keeping emotions under control is required in leadership.
- **Observe your reactions to other people.** Do you stereotype or rush to judgement or are you open and accepting of others' differences and needs?

Simply taking time to reflect on elements such as these means you begin to refocus on the positives and encourage yourself to trust yourself .... We know it's not easy though. It does take practice, and we all know, just as Julia Roberts's character says in Pretty Women, "the bad stuff is easier to believe".

PUTTING A HALT TO FAULTY THINKING

What else do you falsely believe or what other beliefs do you still hold on to that hold you back?

To thrive as our authentic selves, it is necessary to be self-accepting and non-judgemental. Stopping the faulty thinking that hinders self-worth is important, especially for women with tendencies to under-evaluate competencies, stick to guidelines, not ask, wait for deserved rewards or even those experiencing imposter syndrome in senior leadership roles. We need to silence our inner critics.

Remember too that how we reference experiences is also important to understand (76). Internal referencing is related to how an experience feels and it is higher when you want to get things right. If you do this a lot, you are also more inclined to blame yourself more when things go wrong. On the flip side, the externally referencing approach is more related to the impression on others, so you may want to get things right for others so you will be accepted, or even envied by others. Unfortunately, those that lean more to external referencing also tend to blame others when things go wrong. To avoid disappointment or dissatisfaction it can be useful to understand how we reference ourselves, but it must be noted that women are often more internally referencing which can reinforce the inner critic.

Finally, honesty and the ability to admit we are wrong, or we don't know the answer is also important to halt faulty thinking. All too often leaders believe they have to be right, to the extent of justifying or coming up with convenient explanations for their behaviour or to deflect blame.

Remember we can all choose how we think and react.

To dos:
- **Accepting** that no one is perfect, even us, can begin to silence the inner critic and challenge our own referencing.
- Practice **rational thinking** when things go wrong (86). This may mean asking "how important is this on a scale of 1-10? Or will it be important in 6 months? Or what can I learn from this?"
- **Humility** or modesty is also a characteristic worthy in leaders. As CS Lewis said, "humility is not thinking less of yourself, it is thinking of yourself less", qualities required to admit mistakes and show care to others.
- **Apologise** when necessary. Actually saying "I am sorry for..." is not simply a social nicety it helps repair relationships and re-establishes dignity on both sides.
- Practice **forgiveness** as a conscious, intentional and voluntary process to change your feelings or attitude to someone. Others do not need to know that you have forgiven

them; forgiveness is good for *your* emotional health. It starts with expressing yourself (and this does not have to be to the person either), then look for the positives, cultivate empathy towards the other person, finally let go of any anger and move on.

> *The best advice I ever received... Marie Krstic*
> *It was "stay positive" and "focus on doing the right thing". In business we always meet challenges and have to put out fires. Key is not fixing blame but fixing the problem.*

SPACE FOR MINDFULNESS IN THE WORKPLACE

Being in the present is also a powerful way of developing self-belief, emotional health and remaining authentic at work. There is much hype currently on ways to do this with techniques such as mindfulness, however many companies including Google, Deloitte, Deutsche Bank and Siemens, encourage mindfulness in the workplace.

Mindfulness is a practice to focus on the present and can develop positive thinking, focus and clarity of mind. It means being aware of where we are and what we're doing, and not overly reactive or overwhelmed by what's going on around us. Recent scientific research has shown the beneficial effects mindfulness has upon brain activity and training can help people to change the way they think, feel and act. The practice of mindfulness helps to reduce stress, improve working practices and relationships, plus deepens compassion to others.

The practice of mindfulness is a form of meditation, using breathing techniques. This includes awareness of your breathing to connect with experiences or state of mind. By taking time out, even for a few minutes to relax, focus on breathing and simply noticing feelings, observations, or what you are hearing, you can learn to not let your mind wander but accept what is and not compare, judge or criticize. Understanding how things are, not trying to change them, can help letting go, thereby approaching experiences with warmth and kindness, to yourself and others.

"IT'S ALMOST LIKE A REBOOT
FOR YOUR BRAIN AND YOUR SOUL."
(Padmasree Warrior, CTO & Strategy Officer of Cisco Systems, 2008-2015)

MAKING NEW GOOD HABITS

40% of our daily behaviours are automatic with no conscious thought (87). Habits are triggered by cues or specific contexts and often without our awareness, leading to our automatic behaviours. We therefore need to change the cues. To reprogram our unconscious, we need to derail the old, bad habits and use strong new cues to trigger new, better habits. For example, if you always eat a cookie as you enter the kitchen, move the cookie jar! Key is being specific on your goals, getting started, continuing and being kind to yourself. It does take time as the brain needs to re-learn and increase brain cell connection, and for these to stick, they need to be used.

Steps for remodelling our brains and making new connections:

1 **Recognize your willpower supplies**
   Willpower is needed yet it is limited. Willpower diminishes with use, tiredness and stress. It is therefore important to identify when your willpower is ebbing and be conscious of your actions or decisions

2 **Recognize your own triggers**
   If habitual behaviour is automatically triggered by one cue, you need to learn what that is for you. For instance, what is your ingrained reaction to people or situations that you want to change and reflect on what you are reacting to. Is it a compliment that you always respond to in a self-mocking way? Is it a comment on your education that makes you defensive?

3 **Make a clean break**
   Habits are very linked to environment therefore breaking habits or creating news ones can often be easier in times of change, such as starting a new job. This interrupts regular patterns and means the old cues do not trigger you. New contexts also allow the brain to arrange new unconscious behaviours until they too become habits.

4 **Repetition**
   Repeating new behaviour ingrains it and the repetition of conscious responses turns cues and triggers into automatic behaviours.

The best way to learn, retain and over-ride your automatic responses is to focus attention on what you are doing and actively keep recalling it. Slips ups will happen though! Use these as reminders that you still need to reset a cue, so forgive yourself and keep practicing.

WHEN SELF-BELIEF GOES INTO OVER-DRIVE

When we looked at emotional competencies, one point we noted was that **balance** is required. This is based on the fact that our behaviour impacts others. Just because you can handle ambiguity for instance, does not mean others can. As an example, ambiguity tolerance is the capacity to deal with uncertainty, unanticipated change, lack of structure or routine. Yet when it is too high, a person risks becoming bored and may create disorder to keep things stimulating. When it is too low, a person will become anxious and seek to create too much control and structure. A leader with high ambiguity tolerance must remember that when others do not share this, they create an atmosphere of high stress!

Linking back to self-belief, too high self-belief or self-confidence can be perceived as arrogant and with such people they often fail to include others, seek inputs, value different perspectives and certainly not value feedback or criticism. As a word of caution, whenever you find your self-confidence, never confuse this with over-estimating your own importance! **Humility** is what keeps people grounded. It is also what allows us to focus on others and serve them well. It is knowing what you bring to the table, not being afraid to talk about it, nor being afraid to ask for help.

Alongside humility, also challenge your own **expectations** of yourself and others. It is okay not to be Wonder Woman. Towards others, do not hold on to unrealistic demands. Treat all others with respect and as individuals and value what they bring, especially when it differs from your experiences or beliefs.

Finally, be **open to feedback** and when you hear negative comments or resistance to how you do things, it is essential to reflect on them as there is often some element of truth that, if heeded, could improve your performance further. In a recent coaching scenario, a female project manager described a conflict situation with a peer who was feeling excluded from decision making in projects. Her view was that she was including the whole team; his feeling was that she sought information yet made all the decisions herself. Missing advanced collaborative skills and not being able to reflect on the specifics of a collaborative decision-making process, this argument left the woman believing that her colleague was only complaining because she was a woman. When things go wrong, never start from the assumption that it's because you are a woman. Even as a highly successful woman, you can be wrong. Be rational, consider facts, reflect on your actions, put yourself in the shoes of others to understand how they may perceive events differently, even ask for more examples. You can always strive to be better!

- Self-belief is the first enabler to shift the scales for success for women in leadership and it is linked to mindset and attitude

- Self-belief is essential as how we feel and think about ourselves has a strong influence on how we behave and therefore on how we are perceived by others

- Our behaviour in business is not only important as it is how we judged, but also because our actions can directly impact others. Our visible behaviours, such as what we say or do, can be seen in our communication style and this impacts how successful we are when we interact with others

- How we think is all about how we plan, solve problems and make decisions and this impacts how successfully we deliver results

- How we feel in business is translated into emotional intelligence, our ability to understand and manage how we feel to be appropriate in a business setting, as well as how we understand and manage the feelings of others

- High emotional intelligence allows us to be successful in social or stressful situations and this can be learnt. Self-awareness, self-reflection and self-control are necessary to achieve this

- Building self-confidence is essential and linked to our mindset to enhance the way we think about ourselves, and to our mannerisms to transmit a sense of confidence to others

- Learning to stop the negative thinking and creating new positive thinking habits allows us to recover from any false beliefs that hold us back

Chapter Seven

PRESENCE AND IMAGE ARE EVERYTHING

How penguins show power

When penguins greet other penguins or enter an area full of penguins, they use body language to ensure others know they are there. They assume an expansive stance, use strong eye contact and they try to fill the space. This is all about showing physical power and dominance. When displaying dominance, men (and penguins) are perceived positively and considered diligent (88). When we as women behave in a decisive way we are often referred to as being dominant. This is because the expected behaviour of women is to be "nice" yet when we do express more "female" behaviours, we are judged as being less competent and capable (10) ...

Expectations also form another part of visible power: Penguins make up a huge part of governments, boards and executive management. Most are white, middle-class, heterosexual and middle-aged (35). This "default man" has thrived and colonized the high-status, high-power roles because of what he is and because he looks like power (35).

What does this mean for women? Unfortunately, if you want to be part of a crowd, you have to look and act the part. Therefore, creating your own professional business persona is a key step. We also have to learn to use presence and body language to take up space and fill the room!

POSITIVE SIGNALS

Presence relates to our ability to send positive self-signals. Alongside confidence, physical presence and a professional appearance sets the scene and defines the image we project.

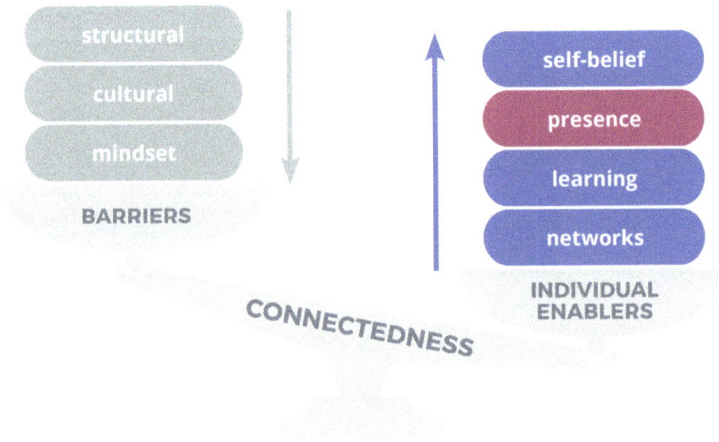

Figure 14: Shifting the scales for success includes individual or personal presence

Our presence, or our bearing, is a personal ability and active mechanism for making our character known to others, including expressing opinions and exerting influence through image, spoken word and body language (4). Presence can also be linked to the emotional competence of composure, and one that affects others and is therefore required in balance. Composure is the ability to remain cool and unflustered in the face of frustrations or difficulties. Yet if too highly composed, you will appear uninvolved, indifferent, or remote, but too low can result in overreacting emotionally and not making sound judgements.

> **The best advice I ever received... Katrin Winkler**
> *As leadership is not about being liked but being respected, I had to learn how best to make strong points and to show less "female behaviour". One of my male ambassadors gave me the feedback that I was overly expressive when presenting and I should adopt a less "emotional" presentation style in formal settings. For me this was key to showing competence and not relying on friendliness to make an impact.*

A PROFESSIONAL BUSINESS PERSONA

The impression we give and the image we create has a strong influence on how we are treated at work and how we are seen as leaders (89). Whether we like it or not, we need a professional business persona for both self-image and as a role model for other women. It is not only what we look like, it is about demonstrating skills and competence, and how we interact. The most highly ranked skills for **professionalism** are communication, with appearance ranking second (89). Even after initial first impressions have passed, and we have interacted with people face-to-face, we continue to be influenced by people's appearance (90). It is our brain's short-cuts again. Behavioural confirmation or self-fulfilling prophecy ensures we look for information which confirms our expectations, and we make a number of other attributions such as associating looks with competency. Furthermore, facial cues are extremely powerful in shaping interactions, even in the presence of other information. All this means we need to be very aware of our appearance, speech and body language, especially in critical first meetings. You need to look the part and "play" the part, in other words; do not diminish your impact. Women have a strong tendency to smile more and express agreement by nodding which can actually have a negative impact. Such "female stereotype behaviour" is often perceived as less competent. So, when you have to make a strong point, adopting a less emotional style and looking more "powerful" makes a difference.

THE FIRST SEVEN SECONDS RULE

In any senior management meeting or in critical first meetings, making a good and memorable first impression is key, and it really does happen in the first 7 seconds (77). So, remember the following:

- **Smile** - Facial expression says more about you than words. Make sure it's real and warm, confident and professional.
- **Shake hands** - The handshake (in non-pandemic times) is the universally accepted signal of professionalism, politeness and confidence. A good handshake is a fine art - a tricky balance between a tight squeeze and a limp stroke. Additionally, if there are several people in the meeting, greet them all separately.
- **Introduce yourself** – Never assume everyone knows who you are, so when you shake hands also say your name.
- **Speak clearly** - Speak in a competent and confident way making sure what you say is relevant and appropriate. Speak slowly and talk at an appropriate pitch - people take others more seriously if they have a deeper voice (sorry ladies).
- **Maintain eye contact** - People are perceived as nervous or rude when they don't make eye contact. Make sure you lock eyes for 4-5 seconds at a time, then look away to avoid stressing the other person.

For women, getting all this right is really tricky. It's the old double bind conundrum again. It is better to aim for professionalism and **professional respect** whenever in doubt. For leaders, the critical link is to build respect. In the book "Winners, and How They Succeed" (91), sports stars, politicians and leaders were examined. What was found was many different approaches and differing styles, but the common factor was that they were respected. For example, when interviewed, Clive Woodward, successful sports coach, was asked if he had to choose between being respected or liked by his players, Woodward responded, "I would go for respect every time".

> **Professional respect is a feeling of deep admiration for someone elicited by their abilities, qualities, or achievements, not for looking cool or being liked.**

THE IMPORTANCE OF APPROPRIATE BODY LANGUAGE

Professional respect comes from who you are, what you do and how you do it. As said, the top two factors for professionalism are appearance and communication skills (89). Yet, when it comes to communication, it does not matter what you say unless it is augmented with appropriate accompanying body language because our receptiveness towards others is not just based on words. Words are only 7% of receptiveness to communication. Tone of voice is 38% and body language is 55% (92). To fully understand how communication works, and especially how misunderstandings may come about, it is important to note that communication is based on meaning and interaction and human communication involves verbal and non-verbal elements. To understand a message properly, both have to be considered (93). When the verbal / non-verbal don't match, this confuses people and makes it difficult to understand the message. Non-verbal communication is much stronger, more intuitive and more difficult to manipulate therefore must be considered for impressions and impact.

- Simple **positive signals** include a real smile, good eye contact, leaning in towards someone, using reaffirming noises such as uh, ya..., and active participation in conversation. All shows warmth and genuine engagement.
- Signals of **losing attention** can include broken eye contact, turning away at 45-90°, slouching, checking a watch or even sighing.
- **Defensive signals** are arms crossed, leaning backwards and a blank face. Further disagreement signals include a set jaw, shaking head sideways and narrowed eyes.

Furthermore, Stanford Professor Deborah Gruenfeld believes that body language is especially **important in power and influence** (88). Research shows that people posed in expansive postures feel more powerful, exhibit higher testosterone levels and have lower levels of the stress hormone cortisol — all characteristics of high-ranking social status. Making eye contact while talking, but feeling free to look away when others do, is called having a high "look-speak to look-listen ratio," which is also common for dominant members of groups. Yet power is not only demonstrated through body language but also by "**filling the room**" – making sure that when you enter a room people know that you are there. Taking ownership of the space around you, means spreading your stuff and claiming territory physically. Penguins do this very well! We need to watch and learn. Gruenfeld recommends saying to yourself "This is my room. This is my table. This is my audience". Also, she says never bother over-explaining yourself, speak succinctly and remember to slow down. And when it comes to the inevitable bind of how to achieve influence without being deemed intimidating and aggressive, Gruenfeld encourages women working in male-dominated environments to consider the duties that come with senior roles and power. "Think of yourself as a protector," she explains. It is about acting with dignity and respect and making other people feel safe, not threatened.

Ultimately, what we are talking about when we talk of presence is a quality that is a blend of image, competencies and interpersonal skills, that when combined well, send all the right signals. It is having the full package of strong **personal brand,** making it clearer for everyone else to know what you stand for. It's a "wow" factor that sets people apart and gives a career that extra boost (5).

We associate branding with products or companies, yet personal branding is important for leaders. A brand is generally considered a name, logo, slogan or design scheme that creates expectations of the product or company and can be described as the promises the supplier is making towards a customer. Ferrari brings a promise of sports car glamour, Audi promises German engineering. Customers build trust in brands they experience or believe in and are willing to try new products just because of this trust. Personal branding is also establishing an impression in the minds of others. It is also a managed process starting from building a professional business persona and delivered consistently throughout a career. It is creating a mark that identifies you and your career and one to use to express values, personality and skills (94).

Michelle Obama

For an example of a strong personal brand, let's consider **Michelle Obama**. She soared into the public eye during her time in office as first lady of USA. Far more than just the wife of the president, this incredible woman established herself as a thought-leader in her own right. The result is a brand that is known throughout the world. Michelle Obama is a globally renowned figure for articulate, engaging, and relevant public speaking (5). But did you know that this positive brand took some work and finessing? Early on when campaigning with her husband, she was perceived to be aggressive. It was only when a communication expert made her watch a video of herself with the sound off that she saw how her dynamic body language could be seen as very forceful and took steps to work on her professional image (95).

SPEECH AND NARRATIVE SUPPORT YOUR PERSONAL BRAND

Communication skills are linked to professionalism and building trust, essential for leaders (4). The goal of communication is not only to inform, but to engage others and build rapport. Beyond speaking clearly, in a competent and confident manner, make sure what you say is relevant and appropriate for the audience, avoiding slang and jargon. Speak slowly, at an appropriate pitch and set a positive tone, in other words, be solution oriented. No one likes moaners. When talking to people one-to-one, show appreciation and ask questions. Genuine dialogue occurs when listening to understand, not listening to interrupt, with the intention of establishing a mutual relationship (4).

Though much of work communication is task related, leaders especially benefit from being able to communicate a **positive personal narrative** because part of who we are is knowing what our story is, giving a sense of identity, hence linked to brand.

How do you tell your story? How do you explain where you come from and how this has shaped you? How do you share what you stand for, your values, your vision and what you bring to the organization? Having the confidence to vocalize who you are may unconsciously influence you to act in a positive way and enables you to think about yourself in an objective way too.

> **It is all about positive self-marketing.**

To create a personal narrative, pitch or a one-minute elevator speech, it has to be simple, starting with a captivating headline, explaining why someone should listen based on the opportunity you bring and challenges you can overcome for them and what outcome will result. All too often we get bogged down with too many details on what we do and how we do it. Learning from communication expert Simon Sinek, he advocates focusing on **the "why" to inspire others** (96). To engage people on a more emotional level, a message must explain the why first. There are two forces that govern human behaviour, why and how. Why is the motive for doing something, the meaning. How is the method of doing it, the part that is objective and detailed. When it comes to engagement and buy-in, motive trumps method, in other words, why trumps how. Easier said than done though as how and what (actions) are simpler and less stressful to talk about in many situations (4).

APPEARANCE AND CLOTHING

Business attire has changed significantly over recent years, yet too many people have forgotten why proper business attire is still important. Though some companies encourage employees to dress casually, others require a more defined and professional dress code to maintain a professional image of the business, especially where employees routinely interact with clients and partners. Conflicts arise when employees dress for comfort or style, rather than realizing the importance of presenting themselves in a more professional manner.

> **How an individual dresses for work can be a powerful extension of personal brand. Clothes, accessories and even the footwear an employee chooses to wear help to reinforce or diminish their skills and qualities in the eyes of their employer (89).**

This may sound old fashioned, especially in today's world of t-shirt-wearing tech CEOs such as Mark Zuckerberg, yet those wishing to build impact and reputation must be cognitive of the **biases, prejudices and stereotypes linking appearance and competency**. If you wish to be taken seriously, dress for it. Dress for the next level, dress for the role you wish. You are unlikely to appear over dressed, rather, seen as a contender. Even if it says, "business casual", always wear a business suit. Especially as a woman in the business world, being absolutely professional at all times includes dress code. It is about adjusting for the situation – it is work, not home life or party time! Even for hairstyles, the key is to look professional again, not beautiful. So maybe it's a bit boring, but no experiments. Same is true for makeup – keep it simple. Jewellery also matters – it finishes off an outfit. And if you want a splash of colour, try a scarf. If it's the same colour as your eyes, it also draws attention to them. And as for stockings or tights. YES! You would laugh if a businessman was not wearing socks, so cover legs at all times. According to recruitment companies and head-hunters, 67% bosses turn down applicants as a result of their inappropriate dress sense (97). Men turning up for interviews with no tie, a t-shirt and jeans were deemed as some of the biggest fashion offences to employers. Women wearing dangly jewellery failed to make the cut and flashing bare legs in mini-skirts also failed to help women land a career, with bosses opting in favour of candidates in mid-length hemlines. The point is, clothes are a way of exerting some control on the sort of attention you receive (35).

So, how to go about designing a **personal dress code**? Although a one-size-fits-all or universal dress code may not be achievable or realistic, some guidelines are possible for those choosing what to wear each day (89):

- **Be modest** - Get attention for great work rather than for wearing the latest fashion fad.
- **Be comfortable** – Think about the fit of your attire, especially the comfort of shoes.
- **Be mindful that basic etiquette must accompany appropriate attire** – This does mean a suitable skirt length and not too revealing tops.
- **Beware of casual Fridays** – These have the potential to turn into fashion disasters. Remember the workweek has not ended and be consistent with every other day of the week.

We really can't say this enough for women! Judgments about you are formed by the way you dress so maintain a standard of dress that creates a positive impression, presenting a professional image of yourself and your company. In the post-COVID-19 world, there has been much speculation about workplace attire, even predictions of the end of the "suited and booted" executive (123). There may well be change, even to the point of more functionality and less formality. However, we want to reiterate the danger that unconscious bias causes for a negative image and the importance of appearance for positive image, and more importantly, self-confidence. Even on a video meeting, you are still in a meeting and need to dress the part – sweat pants and a t-shirt don't do you justice!

Angela Merkel

What comes to mind when you think of **Angela Merkel?** Successful politician? Well respected? Fashion icon? You may be surprised to know that she traveled with a stylist in her entourage, whose task it was to make sure the Merkel look was unchanged, same hair, same makeup, same style. She had a wardrobe of different-coloured jackets and trousers of the same design. It was a deliberate tactic to avoid comment on how she looked rather than inspire, and it reinforced her personal brand of strategic seriousness (91).

"WHEN HE DONS A UNIFORM,
A MAN TAKES ON A BIT OF THE POWER OF ALL
MEN WHO WEAR THAT UNIFORM (35)."

(Grayson Perry, author and artist)

BECOMING A ROLE MODEL

How you dress and how you behave not only risks diminishing your qualities in the eyes of others, but they can also inspire others or reinforce the belief of others in their own abilities or ambitions.

The reality for a leader is that their presence and actions impact others every day. Leaders are looked upon for direction, guidance, even reassurance. The challenge is therefore showing a professional yet authentic persona at all times. For women especially, it is also understanding that you are by default role models for future female leaders! When women miss role models, they can believe that the odds of getting ahead are stacked against them and therefore never even apply for the senior roles. On the other hand, having strong female role models, especially those that advocate for the development and promotion of other women, has been shown to affect attitudes greatly. We are a little bit like penguins too – when we see others like us, we know it is where we can get to too!

WHEN PRESENCE BECOMES DOMINATION

A positive presence needs to radiate authenticity. It is not about charisma, or personality per se, it is about being respected and authentic. Finding a path to **authenticity** takes time but yields strong results. It starts with understanding your own story, your values and even how overcoming difficult experiences can give meaning to life. Authentic leaders have also been shown to work hard at understanding and developing themselves, using formal and informal support networks to get honest feedback and help ground themselves because an individual does not have to be born with any universal characteristics or traits of a leader to learn how to be a successful leader (98).

> "LEADERSHIP HAS MANY VOICES.
> YOU NEED TO BE WHO YOU ARE, NOT TRY
> TO EMULATE SOMEBODY ELSE."
> (Kevin Sharer, CEO of Amgen, 2000-2012)

The critical point of learning to lead and learning to be yourself all too often shows when women get this wrong. We sadly witnessed such an event when a fellow colleague was promoted from within to a C-suite level role, the first woman to hold such a position in this company. The challenge of being the first into such a role is that many eyes are on you, and both men and women will judge, rightly or wrongly, as some look for inevitable mistakes and some look for new role models. Unfortunately, this example did not end well. Once in place, she changed. She started acting as a "man"; dressing in very harsh suits, not listening to others, giving no space for others to shine, and becoming overly dominant. What was even worse was that she began pushing away all those that had helped her develop, and even removed other women who she saw as threating her unique position. She therefore lost her support network, and when the business took a downturn, she had no backup. This highlights that women too need to be authentic and not try to be like men. Successful women are successful on their own terms and need to stay true to this and remember the success factors, which generally include the support of others. More on the importance of networks in chapter 8.

KEY LEARNING POINTS ON PRESENCE AS AN ENABLER

- Presence is the second enabler to shift the scales for success and it is also linked to the perception or image we create which influences how we are seen as a leader

- Presence is physical and it is a personal ability and active mechanism for making our character known to others, including expressing opinions and exerting influence through our image, spoken word and body language

- Women need a professional business persona. This is all about demonstrating skills and competence, how we interact through our communication and our appearance

- We need to make a good first impression, develop professional respect and use appropriate body language. This includes how we "fill the space"

- What we say and how we say it also promotes our personal brand and relates to our own self-marketing

- How we dress for work is an extension of personal brand. Clothes, accessories and footwear help to reinforce or diminish our skills and qualities in the eyes of employers

- Dressing for success involves looking the part, even online!

- The challenge for women is showing a professional yet authentic persona and by default being a role model for future female leaders

Chapter Eight

LEARNING NEVER STOPS

How penguins fail

In Assessment Centres for senior management positions, we often see a very different pattern in men and women when it comes to how failure is attributed. This mirrors how penguins attribute success (see chapter 5). In such settings, men (penguins) show a tendency to attribute failure externally. Usually, and of course not for all, when a male candidate fails in an exercise the first discussion is usually that the exercise was too difficult or that they would react differently in a "normal" situation. The women on the other hand have a tendency to reflect on their missing competencies. This tendency in men in the extreme leads to an overestimation of their own capabilities. Women tend more towards an underestimation of capabilities and the self-fulfilling prophecy of feeling inadequate, questioning abilities and then being perceived as less capable.

START WITH SELF-REFLECTION

Once again, self-reflection is a good thing for individual development and growth yet emanating a positive believe in your own capability is key, as is accepting that failure should not be feared. Learning from penguins, sometimes there are external hindrances to success and sometimes you just have to dust yourself off and carry on. What is important is not to wallow in self-doubt but refocus back on your strengths and what you can do to move forward. And when that doesn't work, you need to go back to rational thinking: what can I learn from this? (86)

> "IDEAS RARELY COME FROM DOING NOTHING.
> WE STIMULATE OUR BRAINS TO COME UP WITH IDEAS
> WHEN WE LEARN NEW THINGS (6)."
>
> (Philippa Perry, psychotherapist and author)

LEARNING KEEPS US HEALTHY

Learning starts from understanding strengths. Learning also allows us to develop our natural aptitudes or natural abilities, into real talents. From learning, whether it be knowledge, skills, competencies or behavioural based, when we have the confidence to apply it, we can make the difference. We just need the ability and willingness to do so. Not only is learning fun, but continuous learning also facilitates success and learning keeps us mentally healthy. Being pushed out of our comfort zones and learning something new promotes brain fitness (6).

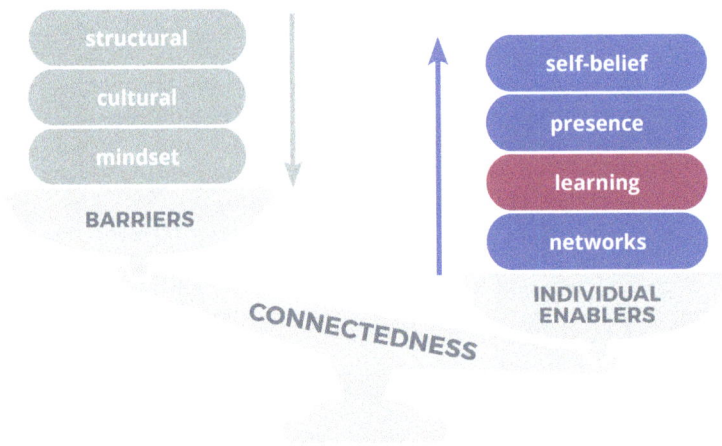

Figure 15: Shifting the scales for success includes individual learning

No one person has all the answers. Curiosity and life-long learning define successful people who strive to be their best. This is not only seen in skills they develop, but also in how they think and approach new challenges. Such people can also be described as **agile learners**:

- Not afraid to admit they don't know it all
- Keen observers
- Look for comparisons
- Can apply lateral thinking or guiding principles
- Can adapt, and keep learning from all situations

Continuous learning is a critical competency for all workers, it is associated with potential for success in new roles and a criterion for top talents. It also links to the cognitive dimension of leadership. What is important to note is that for adults, only an individual can achieve the full learning process. Organizational opportunities or courses can provide experiences and feedback can stimulate self-reflection; yet this and subsequent phases of iterative learning can only come from you! In any setting, you need to think about what went well or what could have been better. These are the eureka moments when you know what to keep doing or change. From here, action is then required! And this adult learning process keeps on going and going.

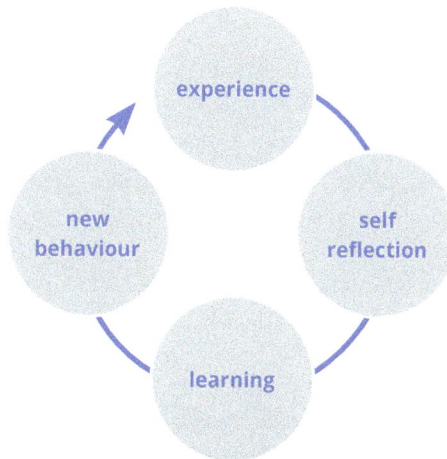

Figure 16: Adult learning process (5)

Learning is ever more poignant for women, and it is important to pay attention to your skills and competencies to succeed as a leader. Remember that male potential (future estimate on being able to do a job) is preferred over female track record (proven performance) (30). Such evidence highlights the need to shout about achievements and be willing to proven time and again that you can do the job. You need the right skills and the right language to demonstrate competency and ability. The best way? Degree up and title up!

The best advice I ever received... Line Raquet
Simple – it was travel, learn and build your experience! Following this advice has made me more open, more willing to listen to others and having exposure to business around the world has meant I understand the broader issues and concerns across geographies and across functions. It has made me a more collaborative CEO.

DEGREE UP!

Continuous learning as a competency describes seeking ways to enhance knowledge and skills and active involvement in learning activities for personal development. It includes facing criticism and learning from mistakes, understanding and dealing with own strengths and development areas, and asking for and using feedback to improve performance. Key is applying newly acquired skills and knowledge in daily work.

So how to learn the right things for leadership success? In reality, it is on the job! The 70/20/10 learning concept (99) highlights the contribution to learning from on the job experiences. 70% of any development plan should include significant elements leveraging new tasks, new projects etc. to expand skills and competencies. 20% is based on the learning relationships we have, such as our role models and mentors. 10% is formal learning. Though 10% sounds low, as a woman, having business qualifications is highly recommended. Developing new skills through professional training and qualifications improves readiness for a leadership role, as well as strengthening a CV. CVs need **qualifications** to give credibility. They also need **experience** in management and leadership roles. The most successful leaders we know have strong resumes that include:
- Qualifications
- Business and leadership courses
- Focus on achievements
- Evidence of competencies shown through examples of challenges, actions and results
- Progressive career steps, with lateral moves across functions for broader views
- International experience

Please don't be put off if your CV does not contain all the above. Please do not fall into the trap of not applying for a role as you are not 100% there. Be a penguin, but also have a plan for filling your gaps over time.

MANAGEMENT AND LEADERSHIP COMPETENCIES

In summary, our recommendations always include building solid experience at work, and this includes in multiple functions and global roles. Also, strive to increasing knowledge at every opportunity and focus on skills and transferable **competencies**. Whereas skills are more often linked to a role or functional area, such as accounting skills or marketing skills, competencies are transferable abilities which enable success in complex and unknown situations (100, 101). Competencies can be developed and strengthened and are important to understand as they have been shown to contribute more than intelligence in determining success. They indicate who is more likely to do a job better, even when skills and knowledge levels may be the same. Competencies can be selected for, used as qualitative performance measures during appraisals, and developed. Many companies create competency models to define the factors they desire in employees. There is often much common ground here as competencies are well researched (100, 101):

- Core competencies: often include elements such as customer or service orientation, taking initiative, teamwork and flexibility. Many companies see these as relevant for everyone and as such, all employees are assessed according to these.
- Entrepreneurial competencies are often used to define the additional expectations of those employees who have strategic or budget responsibility, as these include strategic thinking, decision making and risk taking.
- Leadership competencies are those expected of people managers and include employee performance management linked to goal setting and goal achievement, employee development and change management.
- Meta-competencies transcend all of the above. These are overarching competencies that are relevant to a wide range of work settings and which facilitate adaptation and flexibility on the part of people and therefore organizations. These critical success criteria are learning and communication!

If you remember back to figure 2 in chapter 1, leadership is about balancing task and people aspects of work and inspiring others to be engaged and committed to work and personal success. It is about creating an environment in which others can succeed and going beyond the business management tasks to achieving results through people (5). In terms of skills and competencies, it is also important to understand that you need the management side first, which is all about focus on business performance. Tasks and abilities include defining goals and structures, planning, scheduling work and controlling activities and results. Yet, the responsibilities of leadership include people elements, such as team building and coaching to inspire and motivate others.

	MANAGEMENT	LEADERSHIP
Competencies	• Accountability • Planning & problem solving • Decision making • Strategic thinking & acting • Change management ***Plus for people managers:*** ***Performance management*** ***Employee development***	• Idealized influence (role modelling ethical behaviour) • Inspirational motivation (purpose and direction for others) • Individualized consideration (building up others to contribute) • Intellectual stimulation (leveraging new perspectives and challenging the status quo) • Integrative support (digital connectedness for inclusivity)
Meta-competencies	• Effective communication • Continuous learning	

Figure 17: Key management and leadership competencies

The most effective leadership style, **transformational leadership** (5), balances both a focus on business performance (tasks such as the planning) and people-related actions to create an environment in which all can contribute and succeed. The evidence for the effectiveness of transformational leadership is well established and proven in complex global environments. Furthermore, as women show tendencies to work better in trans-formational cultures, learning how to lead transformationally makes sense! The extended transformation model, also known as the 5 Is, is a model to create an environment of trust and includes the leadership competencies in figure 17:

- Idealized influence (how leaders need to role model ethical behaviour)
- Inspirational motivation (how to share purpose and provide direction for others)
- Individualized consideration (how to get the best from others by building up others to contribute)
- Intellectual stimulation (how to create a thinking environment, leveraging new perspectives and challenging the status quo)
- Integrative support (how to work with remote teams or partners through digital connect-edness for effective inclusivity)

If you would like to learn more about this model, we recommend our book "Connected-ness: Leadership for a Changing World" (5).

Many of the leadership qualities in the transformational leadership model align well with emotional competencies that women have been shown to demonstrate better than men.

As discussed in chapter 1, "women outperform men in 11 of 12 key emotional intelligence competencies crucial for effective leadership". Women demonstrate better self-awareness, empathy, coaching and mentoring, influence, inspiration, conflict management, organizational awareness, adaptability, teamwork and achievement orientation (7). This is a great starting point for a new world of collaborative business, yet we stress the need to also have the skills to deliver business results. If you think that being nice to people will bring success, you are wrong. Being Ms Nice only breeds mediocrity. Yes, cake on Fridays is fun and your team will rate you highly at the beginning, but if you do not enable people to succeed, they will in time be demotivated and leave. Success is linked to personal and business achievement with fun!

GET YOURSELF MENTORS

As the 70/20/10 learning concept shows, 20% of learning comes from the relationships and interactions you have with people (99). This can include working with role models, being part of networks, and coaching and mentoring activities.

Just to be clear, coaching and mentoring are not the same thing (102). Though both are learning methodologies, **coaching** requires a coach to step back and allow the other person to find their way and acting as a coach in a business setting is facilitating learning. Coaching is focused on a current skill or competency gap related to current job or tasks or near job.

Mentoring on the other hand is future oriented, considering a person's path forward and as such can look at broader competency expansion such as leadership skills. A mentor can be a colleague, but one who has an emotional investment, can share personal experiences and offer advice on how they would approach a situation. As such they can be inspiring as a role model. They can also open doors, give access to new networks. It is about growth.

Learning method:	COACHING	MENTORING
The question	How?	What?
The focus	The present	The future
Aim	Improving skills	Developing and committing to learning goals
Objective	Raising competence	Opening horizons

Figure 18: Coaching versus Mentoring

Mentorship is as old as time but often overused and under whelming. It can be a powerful tool for career development, benefiting both individuals and organizations, and it is one of the essential requirements to aid the paradigm shift for improving diversity and women in leadership.

"SHOW ME A SUCCESSFUL INDIVIDUAL AND I'LL SHOW YOU SOMEONE WHO HAD REAL POSITIVE INFLUENCES IN HIS OR HER LIFE... A MENTOR."

(Denzel Washington, actor)

As said, mentorship is as old as time. The origin of the term "mentoring" lies in Greek mythology and The Odyssey. Odysseus asked his friend Mentor to take care of his son during his absence, to prepare him for his future role as king. Derived from that story, "mentor" means teacher, educator and role model. In the current understanding the mentor´s function is to allow the mentee to benefit from their experiences and to accompany the individual career development of the mentee. The focus lies on generating new or broader perspectives, developing strategic approaches, implementing new behaviours and gaining access to networks. Within an organization, mentorship and championing of talented individuals increases exposure to senior leaders, shapes development and prepares people better for new roles. Mentorships provide a safe environment to share issues related to professional and personal success. As it is also based on trust, respect and care, it is generally a long-term relationship.

We cannot make this point strongly enough - we recommend that all individuals, especially those with leadership designs, **actively seek out mentors for learning and for career development**! Especially for women, the need for mentors is profound. McKinsey data (24) shows that senior managers' actions have a big impact, both on a woman's career progression and level of ambition. Women are more likely to be promoted when managers advocate for them, give them stretch assignments, and advise them on how to advance.

When seeking out a mentor, consideration should include finding those who can help with the following (103):
- Broadening perspectives
- Listening, giving feedback, offering valuable opinions
- Giving access to networks to increase visibility within the company or increasing access to knowledge
- Sharing information and experiences
- Offering shadowing, such as observing meetings and providing feedback
- Recommending what and how to learn

There are many examples of the benefits mentees receive from mentoring, and specifically when mentoring is utilized for objective career planning and development, impact on career success, such as promotion and increased compensation, is reported. For example, mentees being promoted 5 times more often than those not in a program (104). It is this specific **career mentoring** that focuses on sharing access and new perspectives such as advice, guidance and opinions (105). It can touch on some elements of coaching to develop the tools to improve skills or competencies needed to get to the next level. What is key is having a highly active mentor, based on the mentor buying in to your potential. Other gains include increased self-confidence and motivation, clear sense of personal direction, as well as opportunity to develop.

There is a slightly different form of mentoring know as **psychosocial mentoring**. In this, mentees also gain more job satisfaction in general (105). Such an encouraging mentoring relationship may not result in direct career development but more emotional wellbeing and increased self-confidence, as well as a sounding board to discuss ideas and approaches before action is taken and an opportunity to think about things in a different way. In this approach the mentor is behaving more as a role model by leading by example, supporting with guidance and confirmation and offering friendship. There may be more elements to enhance self-awareness and self-reflection and such mentoring is often highly rated by mentees.

> ## "HAVING SOMEONE IN YOUR CORNER [WHO]… IS PREPARED TO GIVE YOU THAT GUIDANCE TO GET THERE CAN HAVE A HUGE IMPACT ON YOUR CAREER."
> (Claudine Adeyemi, lawyer)

Mentoring has proven to be a highly effective technique to allow more diverse employees to grow their networks and develop their careers (106). Mentorship can also prepare women for leadership. At the critical step from entry level to management roles, men are still promoted more than women leading to a gender gap at senior levels (24). Not only do talented women need to be promoted to every management level, preparation for senior roles through systematic executive development is key, and for this, the need for mentors is also profound.

In a 2018 interview in the Financial Times, Leena Nair, Chief HR Officer at Unilever, was also clear on the benefits of mentorship for women (107). She believes that "as well as encouraging ambition, they often give access to a wider range of contacts…particularly in organizational cultures where women might not have the same opportunities as men to expand their networks,". She also noted, "women who are mentored have a higher chance of being appointed into senior roles" at Unilever.

So, not only should women actively seek out mentors, other solutions to leverage this unique part of learning and development include investment in formal mentoring and even going as far as **sponsorship of women**, particularly by influential male leaders, to help aspiring women gain the perspective and connections needed to take on larger roles and advance their careers.

	MENTOR	SPONSOR
Level	Experienced person at any level	Senior leader in the organization
Goal of relationship	Provides guidance for career choices and decisions	Uses influence to help you obtain high-visibility assignments or roles
Who drives the relationship?	Both you and your mentor, with your mentor responsive to your needs	Your sponsor chooses to advocate for you, including behind closed doors with other leaders
Actions	Mentor helps you determine paths to meet specific career goals	Advocates for your advancement; champions your potential; opens doors...

Figure 19: The difference with sponsors (50)

While both mentors and sponsors guide professional development, sponsors go further as they are advocates who actively work to advance your career. This means they shout about your accomplishments and potential, as well as recommending you for bigger roles. They are also known to actively help advance career progression through off-the-record or closed-door meetings with other leaders. Sponsors can achieve this by having authority, being a person in power. Today however, that means that in most organizations, this pool of influential sponsors is still primarily male (50). It is why it can be seen more favourable for penguins.... So, while sponsors are important for men, they are critical for women.

In chapter 6, we highlighted the need for self-marketing, because you speaking up about your accomplishments demonstrates confidence. Having a sponsor who speaks up about you is about credibility, it is having someone else vouch for your ability and this really counts!

BE BOLD AND SEEK A MALE SPONSOR

If you want to make it to the top, you will need help. You need self-belief, presence, ongoing learning, and you need others to speak up for you, not just because women tend not to speak up about accomplishments, but because sponsors help you open the doors, rather than you always having to bang them down.

The challenge is that since people naturally tend to gravitate to other people who are like them, male leaders may unconsciously be inclined to mentor and champion other men (50). There is also evidence that for a man to do a woman a favour, he usually needs to know her well enough to feel completely confident in her abilities (39). This means you do need to be bold to access the people (men) who can support you for career advancement, be open with them and show them how good you really are.

The good news is that there are men out there willing and able to sponsor women. We have been extremely fortunate in our careers to benefit from such support, but it is also worth pointing out that the benefits go both ways. Men in leadership roles can strengthen the leadership pipeline in their organizations by helping to retain and advance talented women. Not only do they receive recognition for increasing diversity (106), but they also achieve enhanced perception of their leadership by others. There are also examples of sponsors having greater sense of well-being, including increased job and personal satisfaction (50).

Business today is about inclusiveness for success. Beyond emotional support, people, especially mentors and sponsors, are important for mutually beneficial relationships to exchange ideas, build knowledge, make new contacts, stay current, solve problems and increase morale. Simply spending time with optimistic and successful people has a positive knock-on effect on both parties, so try it out – reach out to others to move up and one day, reach out to help others up.

MOVING UP THE LADDER

What is clear is that leadership starts from you. Throughout a career or within an organization, leaders' responsibility and scope may expand from simply working in a team to managing and developing teams. The focus and tasks may differ, yet the foundation is the individual leader – your knowledge, skills, competencies, behaviours, attitudes, motives and values. As such, leaders must always continue to learn and grow both their business skills and competencies in order to be promoted. The biggest hurdle for women however is how to develop when we are not promoted on potential, only performance, especially when trying to take the first step into a management role. The big question is therefore **how to ensure the first step into management**?

Firstly, **mindset counts** and self-imposed barriers have to go. You have to be positive about your competencies and abilities and know personal strengths. Then, you need to be brave and apply for jobs to put more women in the mix. Learning to speak up for yourself includes speaking to senior managers, HR, recruiters and networks about opportunities. By being direct or even bold about ambition and accomplishments means more influencers are aware of your willingness and desire to move up the ladder.

Secondly, **career development needs to be action oriented**. It starts from understanding personal objectives and expectations of management roles. Showing initiative, taking on more responsibility, even supporting a current manager indicates willingness and can provide on the job development. As said, developing new skills through professional training and qualifications improves readiness for a new role, as well as strengthening your CV. And when seeking internal promotion, demonstrating leadership competencies in a current role or any projects also ensures senior people have evidence of your broader abilities. Then, when actually applying for a management role, quantify proven successes with data, as senior leaders care about candidate achievements and outcomes.

Thirdly, **always over-deliver** in any current role. Hiring managers look for high performance and high potential. Knowing potential is often overlooked for women, you need to show consistent performance that exceeds expectations in any role. Looking back, we have both reflected on the fact that we were doing the more senior job before we were promoted to the position officially. Most organizations are happy for people to step up, take initiative and be accountable. Don't wait to be asked.

Lastly however, based on our personal learnings, whenever you do take on more responsibility or are promoted to a new position, make sure you get the commensurate salary and title. Title up goes alongside our degree up message. When you have the title, you also gain credibility and evidence of success. It makes sure you are seen as competent. When you have the salary, you also have the evidence of responsibility and recognition of your contribution. You also avoid the gender pay gap widening. If you still feel unsure about asking for such fair treatment, remember penguins ask or see chapter 2.

ACTIVE CAREER MANAGEMENT

When you become aware of your talents or strengths, through measurement, feedback and reflection, you have a strong position from which to develop. When you combine this with understanding your ambition, you can start to explore your career options.
Career management is the process that involves career exploration, development of career goals, and use of career strategies to obtain career goals. This can be individually driven and augmented with leadership support with mentors and sponsors. For the individ-

ual side, career planning is the process of making and implementing informed decisions, starting from:

1 Defining what pieces you already have in place:
   • What is your current position?
   • What are your strengths to leverage (skills & competencies)?
   • What are your qualifications?
   • What experiences have you gained?
   • What are your personal values that are important in your work?
   • What is the strength of your network?
   • What are your career goals for the next 3-5 years?

2 Defining a development plan to close any gaps in skills, competencies, qualifications, experience or support networks to prepare you for your ideal future role:
   • Be specific on objectives, expected outcomes and the actions you will take and when
   • Use mixed learning methods – on the job (such as new tasks or projects), working with others (coaching, mentoring and sponsorship) and formal programs (such as courses for knowledge gaps)

WHEN LEARNING STOPS, CONTROL TAKES OVER

Learning how to lead effectively is a daily challenge. It is the constant building of knowledge and experience to be able to show judgement and balance when needed. It is being able to adapt and be relevant at all times, to be stable yet flexible, coherent yet embracing complexity, to deliver consistently high performance whilst ensuring others are still with you. It is also knowing when to reach out and embrace the collective knowledge and experience of those around you. Leadership is never about knowing it all. It is knowing when to ask for help.

As an example, we experienced a leader who was given the opportunity to step up into a much more senior role yet based on her lack of self-awareness and her lack of willingness to keep learning, she approached her new role in a very controlling and narrow way. She assumed she already knew how to be successful so tried to redefine all roles and processes as she had done in the past, in a much smaller setting. She never once considered the new environment or bigger scope that was in front of her and when given feedback, she increased controls and made it her aim to prove she was right. It all became about her winning. Sadly, all she achieved was to destroy a functioning team. The learning here is that **you cannot do it on your own and you cannot always do what you have always done**. The ability and willingness to include others and learn from others is often the best way for overall growth and success.

"THE ONLY MISTAKE YOU CAN MAKE IS NOT ASKING FOR HELP."

(Sandeep Jauhar, doctor and author)

KEY LEARNING POINTS ON LEARNING AS AN ENABLER

- Learning is the third enabler to shift the scales for success and it is also linked to the cognitive elements of leadership and the tools, tasks and skills required to be a leader can be learnt

- Learning keeps our brains healthy and continuous learning is a meta-competence for success in complex and unknown settings

- Adult-based learning is an iterative process from experience to self-reflection, learning and application

- Learning is ever more poignant for women, and it is important to pay attention to skills and competencies to prove credibility and performance, especially as women are seldom promoted on potential

- Degree up, title up and build a strong CV / resume to demonstrate all key management and leadership competencies

- Actively seek out mentors for learning and for career development

- Be bold and seek out a senior male sponsor as advocate for your progression

- Have a plan for career management to explore paths and options, develop career goals, and be specific on how you will keep learning all the way to obtaining those goals

Chapter Nine

PERPETUATING THE NETWORK

How penguins build
alliances

Penguins like to form alliances (108). They are willing to do business with anyone, even someone they don't necessarily like, as long as that person can help them achieve their goals. It is the understanding that this is a work relationship that can be dissolved when it's no longer convenient, not a long-term friendship, that differentiates their networking from that of women. Men's networks also tend to be larger and broader, which is an advantage because a wider audience provides more opportunity to be introduced to someone that may assist with career advancement. Also, in general, penguins network with a clear goal in mind, they are focused on short-term needs and are more comfortable asking for what they want.

NETWORKING

What can we learn from this? We need to get better at networking! There are two elements to consider. Firstly, the world has not changed sufficiently enough that the old saying "who you know" is no longer important. Secondly, despite the social media revolution, we are more isolated than ever and in global business, despite ever more communication technology, management distance has increased. It means that when you make it, it is still lonely at the top unless you have support. Both these elements mean that women especially need new competencies in active networking abilities.

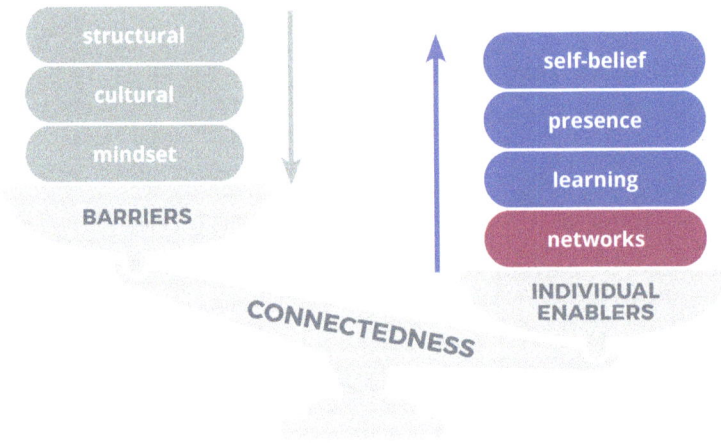

Figure 20: Shifting the scales for success includes significant networking and individual networking skills

WHO IS IN YOUR SUPPORT NETWORK?

People need people and other people continue to be our best resource for development and staying sane (6). We need people to help us get where we want to go, such as our mentors and sponsors. Even once you make it, constantly striving for performance through inspiring others can be tiring or draining. In addition, the more senior you get, the less feedback you get and during difficult times, you need to draw confidence from elsewhere. So, even at the top, leadership is often thought of as a lonely post, but it does not have to be. Leaders today do better when this thought is replaced with a dedication to collaboration, teamwork and support. Not only should leaders seek to build a team around them (formal or informal) for diversity, to balance personal weaknesses and to challenge thinking, but leaders and those aspiring to get there, also need to cognitively build multiple networks.

Firstly, by a **support network**, we mean people willing and able to prop you up, bolster you and provide a solid foundation. So, ask yourself, who is your support network? Who do you have fluid two-way relationships with where you interact freely and comfortably? Who can provide invaluable advice, question, listen, and share hopes and dreams? Such people can be family, friends and colleagues separate from direct teams. They may work in other companies or be senior leaders in other industries. They are trusted people and those you can turn to for support when needed. And all leaders need support and need to know when to ask for it.

> *The best advice I ever received... Nicola Bramwell*
> *As a highly independent woman, I needed the reminder to seek support. My mentor was clear that I couldn't do it all alone. Her generosity was boundless. She gave me the courage to ask for help and in turn, I learnt how I can support others to succeed too. It's why I love working with others. We all grow in the process.*

ENGAGING IN BUSINESS NETWORKING

Beyond emotional support, other **business networks** are also important. Networking is the establishment of mutually beneficial relationships with other people to exchange ideas and build knowledge. This exchange of information includes leaders actively seeking new ideas or broader perspectives from within an organization or from outside. Other benefits are:

- **New contacts** - Meeting potential clients or identifying opportunities for partnerships, joint ventures, or new areas of expansion for the business.
- **Visibility** – Communicating with partners on a regular basis to maintain business relationships.
- **Staying current** - Keeping up with market conditions and overall industry trends.
- **Problem solving** - Finding solutions to business problems or needs, including finding candidates for roles or investment.
- **Confidence and morale** – a boost from spending time with optimistic and successful people.

Networks can be internal or external, formal or informal. Activity relies on effective communication skills and a mindset believing that networking is an important task for leaders, requiring the allocation of sufficient time and effort to see it pay off. If you are to invest time in building networks, face-to-face or online in our new world, key considerations include deciding which networks to reach out to and what skills are required for effective networking.

To improve overall connectedness, four dimensions can be considered; the size, strength, pattern and resources available (109). Size refers to the number of members in the network. Strength of relationships, both strong and weak, are of importance. The pattern of relationships looks at connecting with people outside normal groups and expanding to other communities. Finally, the resources dimension is about determining which connections are useful and deciding which connections are beneficial to both parties.

SIZE

Having a larger friendship network is positively related to social integration, increased organizational knowledge and task mastery. Building and maintaining relationships with others results in a larger network that individuals can turn to for social support, ideas, advice or sponsorship. Networking behaviours to help increase and maintain network size:

- Increase internal visibility, actively engaging in conversations in videoconferences and in person
- Engage in professional activities
- Participate in social gatherings and events
- Maintain contact with others by keeping in touch, such as monthly lunches and coffee

Getting started: Begin with connecting with people you know first. When connecting with people you do not yet know, start with what you may have in common.

STRENGTH

The strength of a connection in a network can be assessed based on the frequency of contact, degree of intimacy, and emotional investment, with weak ties on one end of the continuum and strong ties on the other (110). Both weak and strong ties can be very useful:

- Acquaintances can be more useful for finding jobs as they are a source of more unique information (close contacts tend to know about similar openings)
- Strong ties are often necessary for obtaining complex information (110). Strong relationships may be more important for the transfer of sensitive or complex information than weak ones due to the higher risk and effort involved (111).

PATTERN

The pattern of relationships determines whether the members of an individual network are connected to one another. A gap in a network exists when there is no connection between two members. Most professionals build their network over time through proximity — most work in the same field or industry, are people from business school or colleagues from a current company or past jobs. Most have few outliers in the mix unless deliberate about networking. Also, men tend to network with other men and women network with other women (39). Members who do not know each other are more likely to provide diverse information so try to connect with people outside of typical circles of acquaintances (112). Such reach is easily facilitated online and professional organizations and tools such as LinkedIn can be leveraged. To diversify:

- Make an inventory of existing connections - think about where a network is closed and where there are opportunities to diversify
- Put networking on the schedule
- Ask for recommendations
- Be in it for the long term to fulfil personal curiosity and develop personally. Professional return is a happy coincidence

RESOURCES

The resources or usefulness of a network are the benefits that can be derived from the relationships. Resources can be in the form of information and ideas, social support, job search assistance or business assistance such as providing leads or access to resources. It is not about connecting with someone specifically to gain favour; it is recognizing what resources you and others have and what resources you could share that might be useful and therefore create mutual benefit.

Determining the usefulness of a relationship is about making the right connections, trying to avoid wasting someone's time and recognizing when to strengthen a relationship and when to let it remain a weak tie. To achieve this, develop a clear picture of good connections and set goals. When reaching out it is very important to have a clear reason why you want to meet a specific person. Also consider what you have to offer. This is about your personal brand:

- What are my strengths, what am I known for?
- What am I passionate about, what sets me apart?
- What would I like to accomplish in my life?
- How do I define success?
- What do I want employers or contacts to remember about me?

Figure 21: Four networking dimensions (4)

Be aware however, that networking as a woman is not as straight forward as it appears!

1 You need to **get comfortable** in broadening your business networks – you have to be at the table... Here are some ways to feel more comfortable building an effective network that you can rely on for career advice (113):

   a. Ask for recommendations - networking is the key to getting selected for stretch assignments that often lead to promotions. It is essential you have links or reach to more senior people and those at high levels

   b. Think of networking as a strategic tool - Understand what role you are hoping for and map out which people you could ask for career advice or for sponsorship

   c. Talk about aspirations – never assume others will know that you are open for new opportunities

   d. Never exclude men - The majority of leadership positions are still held by men and they continue to be the gatekeepers for most stretch assignments and promotions. Men may be better placed to provide instrumental networks based on exchange of information related to opportunities and advancement (39)

   e. Reciprocate and share your network - Be sure to offer to return the favour when you ask for help and be generous to help others too!

2 Broaden your **networks beyond friendships**... Women focus on friendships, especially in mentors (108), so be careful not to confuse friendship and mentorship. Rather than only seeking someone you like, seek someone you can learn from. This avoids the common pitfall of not getting the tough feedback you need to move ahead. The best mentors push and challenge you to also take on projects you might otherwise avoid.

3 You need **a close inner circle of women**... Women who try to only network like men actually do the worst because they are missing one crucial ingredient, a close inner circle of women (108).

THE CLOSE INNER CIRCLE OF WOMAN

Women need multiple networks. We need the emotional support network (often friends), the broad business network (like men) and the close inner circle of women! Research has shown that a close inner circle of women is more likely to provide critical private information on job opportunities and challenges (114), such as equal advancement opportunities or whether an interviewer might ask gender-specific questions and the best way to respond. The research also showed that women who form a strong inner circle with other women who can share career advice are nearly three times more likely to get a better job than women who don't have that support system!

Our own personal experiences and observations also concur with the need for a close inner circle of women as coaches, mentors, sponsors and ambassadors. Not only can such a close circle of trust provide advice, honest feedback and be a great sounding board, it is this circle that all too often will champion other women and even facilitate career progression over the long term. Furthermore, it reduces the concerns of women getting the social pushback when they promote themselves.

What we have sadly encountered however is often a lack of loyalty from women who have been developed and subsequently promoted to the senior ranks. In our experience, though penguins are known to network for short term gain, many are very loyal and more open to recognizing the support of others throughout their careers.

QUEEN BEE SYNDROME

The term "queen bee syndrome" is actually a term from the 1970s used to describe mid-level women feeling a lack of support from more senior women. According to Professor Shaun Andrews, there are several reasons why women don't always support other women (115):

Firstly, women at higher leadership levels often display more male-specific **emotional intelligence** competencies, such as assertiveness and confidence, and leverage less female-specific emotional competencies, such as interpersonal relationships and empathy (115). In such cases, if a woman puts less value on relationships, she may not spend the time necessary to cultivate relationships with junior women, hence the queen bee syndrome. It can also occur when women believe they have to behave in ways more typical of men to display toughness, fit in and convince men that they aren't like other women!

A second effect is an unconscious bias that affects the relationship between women when one woman rises in status above another and can cause belittling or even ostracism of the senior woman (115). This is based on a rule in female "culture" that governs relationships. **Power and self-esteem** help shape how women interact with other women at work, as well as in personal lives. For a healthy relationship to be possible between women, self-esteem and power must be equal. When the power balance gets disrupted, such as a woman rising in status, other women may judge and behave unfairly.

A third event can occur when the competition for position within **"in-groups"** increases and here, women have been shown to be less inclined to bring other women along (115), especially when there are few women in an organization or few women in leadership roles.

A fourth observation seen is when the obstacles women have faced in their career have been high and their achievement hard-fought that their attitude toward other women can be "**I figured it out, you should too**" (115). Not a very optimistic or progressive mindset though.

"THERE IS A SPECIAL PLACE IN HELL FOR WOMEN WHO DON'T HELP OTHER WOMEN."

(Madeline Albright, First Female US Secretary of State 1997-2001)

On all of the above explanations, we agree with Madeline Albright! There are too many battles for women without us having to fight other women. Our interactions with other women also help us handle stress better. Under stress penguins go into fight-or-flight mode. Women "tend-and-befriend". We turn to friends in moments of high tension, and this produces a physiological reaction to lower blood pressure, heart rate and cholesterol (9). We are better together!

There is concerning data however that we need to consider and challenge related to **women paying a price for promoting other women** (116) based on how peers view them. In research by the Center for Creative Leadership, they found that women leaders who show that they value diversity in the workplace receive much lower competency ratings than male leaders who show that they value diversity in the workplace. In fact, men's performance ratings actually increase when they show that they value diversity in the workplace, while women's performance ratings decrease. When women promote other women there is the perception of showing favouritism (116). Just one more incorrect assumption we need to ignore or simply document our decisions well to be able to show why we chose the best candidate. Ability and diversity are not mutually exclusive.

BEING A ROLE MODEL NETWORKER AND ADVOCATE

The near-impossible bind of being a woman in leadership takes courage, kindness and strong thinking to question old ways, accepted norms and unfair assessments. It requires us to not only role model great leadership performance but also role model how to network and how to support other women (and good men too).

Best practice collaboration and networking includes active steps to form and participate in networks. It also extends to how you leverage knowledge and insights, for example involving external experts for improvements, visibly engaging with thought-leaders, even having an online presence to share knowledge, both internally and externally.

As a leader, **use your network to help others**, include your team members in your business networks and encourage your team members to participate in new networks for further insights, confidence and learning. In this way, others too will understand the value and benefits of networking.

One final word: Leadership is about people. It is inspiring others to perform at their best. As a successful leader, achieving personal best will have come about because of hard work and the support of many many people. Especially for woman who make it to the top, all the hard work must not be forgotten. Be generous! Be an advocate, share experiences, knowledge and networks with other talented and ambitious women. Be brave and sponsor other women based on yours and their competencies. Be the role model and mentor you may have missed!

"WHEN YOU LOOK AT SUCCESSFUL WOMEN, THEY HAVE OTHER WOMEN WHO HAVE SUPPORTED THEM, AND THEY'VE GOTTEN TO WHERE THEY ARE BECAUSE OF THOSE WOMEN."

(Sheryl Sandberg, COO at Facebook, 2008 to present, and founder of the Lean In organization)

KEY LEARNING POINTS ON NETWORKING AS AN ENABLER

- Networking is the fourth enabler to shift the scales for success for women in leadership. Strong networks are essential for relationships with others and they create an environment that nurtures both ourselves and those around us

- Networking is the establishment of mutually beneficial relationships with other people to exchange ideas and build knowledge, even access new opportunities and career advancement

- Women network differently than men and must pay attention to get this right! Those that try to mimic men often fail here

- Women need emotional support networks, those that provide security often outside the workplace

- Women need broad business networks for reach and these must go beyond "friendships" and must include senior men of influence

- Women must have an inner circle of women – this is the part many miss though these women are more likely to provide critical private information on job opportunities and challenges

- Women must be loyal to those who got them where they are and then must support other women to achieve too. The queen bee syndrome does not have to exist!

Chapter Ten

COPING WITH THE TOUGHER DAYS

How penguins deal with stress

Penguins are problem solvers, but they are focused on performance and competition. They all too often compare themselves to other penguins or demands from penguin hierarchy and they allow this focus to be directed towards winning. The worst "stress" for penguins is the inability to perform, compete or achieve and when confronted by stress, they seek escape. They compartmentalize and repress their feelings in an effort to get away from issues, they change the subject through diversions, such as sports, preferring to hit tennis or golf balls competitively (117)!

STRESS MANAGEMENT AND SELF-MAINTENANCE

What can we learn? Firstly, accept that it is ok to like golf, it's what do penguins do. Secondly, remember that we are not penguins, so we react to stress very differently. For women, our worst stress is a threat to our relationships. These differences are due to brain responses and oxytocin, the hormone released in response to love and one that plays a role in social relationships (118). Men may be more likely to show aggression and react with the **fight-or-flight response under stress**, whereas women show more of a pattern of **tend-and-befriend** (118).

Women are about relationships and our self-esteem and identity are often dependent upon feelings of adequacy in relationships. When confronted by significant "stress", we tend to nurture and reach out to others. We seek support and we talk to lower anxiety and find a solution or answer to problems. When we are feeling unwelcome, always having to bang down doors, keep proving our value or worth, and having to deliver higher performance than men, what we also need to know is how to handle this stress and how to build resilience. Women will often sacrifice their own needs for the needs of others and get caught up in insufficient self-maintenance (119).

Stress is our body's natural short-term reaction to a situation or threat. It is a defensive mechanism, known as the "fight-or-flight response" and can include increased release of stress hormones such as adrenaline and cortisol, increased heart rate, reduced digestion and reduced immune responses. This is because the body is preparing itself. Historically, and evolutionary, the threat was physical attack yet today, stressors are more likely to be mental, emotional or social. It can result in feeling like losing control, anxiousness or being scared (5). There are positive sides to a stress response as stress increases alertness, focus and performance, the challenge is when it goes on too long and hinders performance.

To understand stress, cope with it and build resistance, it is important to consider three elements (120):
- **Stressors** – What is the threat or pressure, real or perceived? In other words, what is the issue?
- **Intensifiers** – What internal processes or faulty thinking are making it worse? Personal attitudes, beliefs (created or inherited), experiences or motives can reinforce the stressor and intensify the problem. Examples include our desire to be perfect, to be strong, to hurry up, to please others, which all make us feel worse.
- **Reactions** – Stress reactions include the physical body changes, emotions, thoughts and behaviours.

Our ability to cope with stress is based on our belief we have the resources to respond to the challenge (121) and our coping resources need to match each of the 3 elements of stress above. Coping needs to include use of three techniques:

- **Instrumental techniques** are required to actually reduce the cause of the stress, for example if constant time pressure is the cause, do you have the necessary time management, prioritization or delegation skills?
- **Mental techniques** are needed to reduce the intensifiers, hence these are all about how you reduce the brain's focus on the problem or improve your attitude. Emotional intelligence, especially self-reflection, is critical here as it provides stability and allows a more realistic assessment of your own reactions, as well as how to deal with others. Mindfulness is a technique proven to work here.
- **Regenerative techniques** reduce the hormone build-up in the body and hence reduce the physical reactions. Exercise or singing makes a difference here!

"EVERY THOUGHT YOU PRODUCE, ANYTHING YOU SAY, ANY ACTION YOU DO; IT BEARS YOU SIGNATURE"

(Thich Nhat Hanh, Vietnamese monk and author)

Stress is inevitable, especially as a leader or when trying to navigate your way up the corporate ladder. What is important is staying true to yourself and showing integrity. It is knowing how to keep stress as a short-term reaction, how to work with the combination of techniques above and how to avoid adding pressure unduly on yourself and others. If your reaction is more along the tend-and-befriend route, also think about avoiding extremes that jeopardize your personal wellbeing. Make sure you know how to set boundaries.

Personal boundaries are your own rules or limits that you need to set to identify reasonable, safe and permissible ways for other people to behave towards you. You also need to decide how you will respond when someone passes those limits. If you have healthy boundaries, you are better placed to be authentic yet balance what you share of your personal information in the workplace. You will be able to understand your personal needs, be willing and able to speak your mind and ask for what you need. You will also have the confidence to value your own opinions and voice these too. You will also be willing to say no and respect when others tell you no. It comes down to personal integrity, not looking for perfection in ourselves or others.

RESILIENCE FOR PERSONAL STABILITY

Our personal ability to regulate our emotional response to stress varies and what is also worth considering is how you build resilience for long-term personal stability (122). Resilience is about coping with situations and not feeling overwhelmed by whatever we must deal with and growing whilst going through whatever life throws at us.

STRESS MANAGEMENT

RESILIENCE

The capacity to recover quickly from difficulties, to "spring back into shape".

stress

Stress is a normal short term reaction to a situation or threat.

anxiety

Anxiety is long term worry, triggered by stress that remains when the threat has gone and impacts functioning.

depression

Severe anxiety associated with suicidal thoughts.

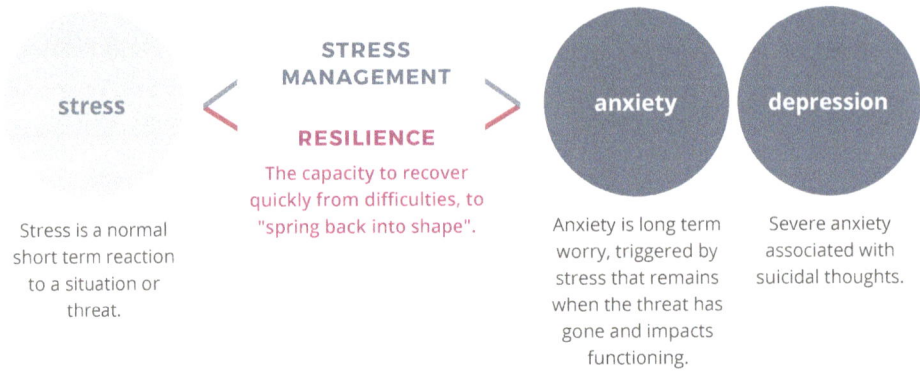

Figure 22: The importance of stress management and resilience (5)

Resilience is the capacity to recover quickly from difficulties. To build resilience, there are seven pillars which you need for the inner strength to keep going and there is much overlap with the leadership development concepts we have already explored:

Self-responsibility	To be accountable for who you are and what you do, acting with integrity, self-confidence and **self-belief**
Self-regulation	To abandon the victim role, showing **presence** and **learning** from all experiences, good or bad
Optimism	To be a **role model** with a positive mindset and attitude to overcome bias and roadblocks
Strong relationships	To leverage the power of **networks** for yourself and to develop other women (and men) by mentoring and sponsoring them
Solution focus	To set goals, focus on business performance and ask yourself, "what can I do about it" to make the difference
Acceptance	To let go of what you can't change when it comes to structural or cultural barriers
Future focus	To create a vision of success for yourself and others, and plan how to get there together

In summary, we are reflecting on how to find balance and fulfilment in leadership. It all comes down to a solid, value-based, non-ego driven foundation for "self" that enables you to act with authenticity and integrity. Such a base allows you to connect with and show kindness to others, at all times and especially when it matters the most. It allows you to question old beliefs and challenge imagined orders and define a new type of business world.

DEALING WITH DIFFERENT PENGUINS

It is not easy being a woman in the male-defined business world. It is not easy being harshly judged. It is not easy having to be better than male counterparts. It is also not easy to always deal with different penguins.

Penguins come in different forms and with different personalities. This is no different in senior management. Some are more open to support women than others, some are more open full stop. Key is remembering that in business, you are not out to make friends, rather you need to achieve **professional respect** for who you are and what you deliver. How you approach and interact with different people or penguins to be seen as credible and professional comes down to your emotional intelligence and your communication style and skill set.

Having a **high emotional intelligence** gives understanding of self and others, tolerance and the willingness to reach out and connect with others, even those who are different to us. As discussed in chapter 5, development of this aspect for great leadership is essential, so make this part of your personal development plan.

Having **strong communication skills** and a toolbox of skills affects how you can adapt and deal with challenging situations, challenging people, as well as disagreement and conflict. What is important to remember is that different viewpoints or perspectives are a good thing! This is the power of diversity and it brings about new ideas and innovations. So, don't shy away from different. Real conflict is way beyond simple differences of opinion or heated discussions. Conflict is serious disagreement often arising from a clash of interests, objectives or values. It can be caused by poor communication, mistrust, attitude or lack of honesty. With openness, with development of the four cornerstones of leadership, and with resilience, you can find the courage speak up and step forward to lead others. So, alongside the development of your management and leadership competencies, invest in development of effective communication.

Lastly, one comment in a women in leadership blog made us laugh as it related to faking it till you make it.... In the long run, it is not the best strategy yet sometimes pretending to be a penguin in a penguin world is a start. Imitating confidence and competence may well be the door opener you need at some point until you know you have it for real!

"ONE OF THE CRITICISMS I'VE FACED OVER THE YEARS IS THAT
I'M NOT AGGRESSIVE ENOUGH OR ASSERTIVE ENOUGH OR MAYBE
SOMEHOW, BECAUSE I'M EMPATHETIC, IT MEANS I'M WEAK.
I TOTALLY REBEL AGAINST THAT. I REFUSE TO BELIEVE THAT YOU
CANNOT BE BOTH COMPASSIONATE AND STRONG."

(Jacinda Ardern, Prime Minister of New Zealand)

A FINAL NOTE

No matter the industry, business or organization, for teams to be engaged, committed and perform at their best and then achieve objectives, they need:
- role models
- inspiring goals
- all individuals working to their strengths
- everyone contributing to improvements
- use of every possible means of inclusion to achieve team spirit and shared purpose

All these points define transformational leadership (5). The latter four are related to what leaders do shape the activities and efforts of people towards joint success. The first point comes back to who you are. To succeed as a woman in leadership, you need to be the best you can be, to role model great leadership for others. What we have looked at here is how to develop to be the best form of yourself through understanding and cultivating four key aspects of leadership and four aspects that can help address gender imbalance:

- Through challenging your own mindset and building **self-belief** and self-confidence, it is possible to over-come any imposter syndrome or inability to ask for what you need
- By holding up a mirror and considering your **presence** and professional image you can send reassuring signals to others that you are confident, credible, competent and authentic. You can also be proud and shout about your achievements and do some self-marketing
- Investment in continuous **learning** helps pinpoint the skills, knowledge, competencies and experience you need to backup ambition with proven success. An openness to take learnings from any event also puts you in a better place to handle inevitable errors or failures. Openness to learning from others leverages the necessary relationship with mentors and sponsors
- Continuing to expand your **networks** for personal growth and to nurture other ambitious people means we can lift up more women, and men, to create more positive environments where everyone can succeed. Networks, both emotional, business and the inner circle of other women also help you find strength and courage to keep going

The glass ceiling may continue to hinder women for the foreseeable future and we will also have to keep proving our value more often than seems fair, yet it is important to remember that whenever women succeed, they can continue to change the roadmap for others. What is important is being at the table and making sure other talented women are present too. There are opportunities out there and there are many organizations receptive to all competent professionals willing to make a difference. What you need to do is use your confidence and aptitude and keep banging down the doors, don't just knock quietly!

"IF YOUR ACTIONS CREATE A LEGACY THAT INSPIRES OTHERS TO DREAM MORE, LEARN MORE, DO MORE AND BECOME MORE, THEN, YOU ARE AN EXCELLENT LEADER."

(Dolly Parton, singer and songwriter)

BIBLIOGRAPHY

All of our concepts and application over many years, are based firmly in academic studies. However, our experiences of working in global companies have also led us to adapt and develop much of the learnings, models and ideas we have shared here. This bibliography is intended to be as accurate as possible for original sources and the thinking of other experts. We do want to make it clear though that what we have found to work, and therefore used in this book, often blends multiple concepts and we apologise sincerely if, and when, we mis-quote or modify ideas beyond their original intention. Leadership is iterative and finding what works for women is also about finding what works for you and what works in the given situation. If there was only one way, it would be easy and there is certainly no one path for women! What we hope we have shown is that being a successful female leader is something you can learn to do better every day. It simply starts with choosing to care about what you do, how you come across and how you want to impact others.

(1)   Hinchliffe, Emma. (2020). The number of female CEOs in the Fortune 500 hits an all-time record. https://fortune.com/2020/05/18/women-ceos-fortune-500-2020/

(2)   Baumeister R.F. (2010). Is there anything good about men - How cultures flourish by exploiting men. Oxford: University Press.

(3)   McGregor, Douglas M. (1960). The Human Side of Enterprise. New York, McGraw-Hill Book Company, Inc.,

(4)   Winkler, Katrin & Bramwell, Nicola. (2021). Connecting and Influencing. A Leader's Guide to Genuine Communication. Linchpin Books.

(5)   Winkler, Katrin & Bramwell, Nicola. (2020). Connectedness. Leadership for a Changing World. Linchpin Books.

(6)   Perry, Philippa. (2012). How To Stay Sane. MacMillan Publishers Ltd.

(7)   Hays Group Report. (2016). Women Outperform Men in 11 of 12 Key Emotional Intelligence Competencies. Hay Group division of Korn Ferry. https://www.kornferry.com/press/new-research-shows-women-are-better-at-using-soft-skills-crucial-for-effective-leadership

(8)   Dr Wayne W. Dyer was an internationally renowned author and speaker in the field of self-development. His latter works emphasised living with purpose and happiness, including The Shift: Taking Your Life From Ambition to Meaning (2010). Hay House Inc.

(9)   Kindersley, Tania & Vine, Sarah. (2009). Backwards in High Heels – the impossible art of being female. Fourth Estate, Harper Collins Publishers.

(10)   Catalyst. (2007). The Double-Bind Dilemma for Women in Leadership. Damned if you do, Doomed if you don't. https://www.catalyst.org/research/the-double-bind-dilemma-for-women-in-leadership-damned-if-you-do-doomed-if-you-dont/

(11)   Blanchard, K. (2011). https://leadingwithtrust.com/category/circles-of-trust/

(12)   Elting, L. (2018). How To Navigate A Boys' Club Culture. Forbes.com https://www.forbes.com/sites/lizelting/2018/07/27/how-to-navigate-a-boys-club-culture/#43ea87264025

(13)   Hamel, Gary. (2007). The Future of Management. Harvard Business School Press.

(14)   Janis, I. (1982). Groupthink. 2nd edition. Houghton Mifflin: Boston.

(15)   Lovegrove, Harley. (2010). Inspirational Leadership: The Five Essential Elements. Linchpin Books.

(16)   Hewlett, S., Marshall, M.; Sherbin, L. (2013). How Diversity can drive Innovation. Harvard Business Review. December 2013. https://hbr.org/2013/12/how-diversity-can-drive-innovation

(17)   Hunt, V.; Layton, D.; Prince, S. (2015). Diversity Matters. McKinsey & Company. Feb 2015. https://www.mckinsey.com/~/media/mckinsey/business%20functions/organization/our%20insights/ why%20diversity%20matters/diversity%20matters.ashx

(18)   Levine, S. & Stark, D. (2015). Diversity Makes You Brighter, The New York Times, Dec 2015. www.nytimes.com/2015/12/09/opinion/diversity-makes-you-brighter.html?_r=0

(19)   Herring, Cedric. (2009). Does Diversity Pay?: Race, Gender, and the Business Case for Diversity. American Sociological Review. Volume 72(2), 2009.

(20)   Goleman, Daniel quote in Korn Ferry article (2016). Source: New Research Shows Women Are Better at Using Soft Skills Crucial for Effective Leadership and Superior Business Performance, Finds Korn Ferry. https://www.kornferry.com/about-us/press/new-research-shows-women-are-better-at-using-soft-skills-crucial-for-effective-leadership. March 2016.

(21)   Erpenbeck, J. & Von Rosenstiel, L. (2003). Handbuch Kompetenzmessung. Stuttgart: Schäffer-Poeschel.

(22)   Management Today (2018). Britain's Most Admired Leaders 2018 are Carolyn McCall and Emma Walmsley. https://www.managementtoday.co.uk/britains-admired-leaders-2018-caro-lyn-mccall-emma-walmsley/leadership-lessons/article/1520261

(23)   Blake, R., Mouton, J., Bidwell, A. (1962): Managerial grid. In: Advanced Management - Office Executive, Vol 1(9), 1962, 12-15.

(24)   Krivkovich, A.; Robinson, K.; Starikova, I.; Valentino, R.; Yee, L. (2017) Women in the Workplace McKinsey Survey October 2017 Report, from https://www.mckinsey.com/featured-insights/ gender-equality/women-in-the-workplace-2017

(25)   Gavett, G. (2017). What Research Tells Us About How Women Are Treated at Work. Harvard Business Review. December 27, 2017 https://hbr.org/2017/12/what-research-tells-us-about-how-women-are-treated-at-work

(26)   Office of the United Nations High Commission for Human Rights https://www.ohchr.org/EN/ Issues/Women/WRGS/Pages/GenderStereotypes.aspx

(27)   Gender Equality Commission of the Council of Europe (2015). Gender Equality Glossary. http://www.coe.int/t/DGHL/STANDARDSETTING/EQUALITY/06resources/Glossarie...

(28)   Gerdeman, D. (2017). Why Employers Favor Men. Harvard Business School Working Knowl-edge. 11 Sep 2017. https://hbswk.hbs.edu/item/why-employers-favor-men

(29)   McKinsey (2011). Unlocking the Full Potential of Women in the US Economy. Special report for The Wall Street Journal. https://www.mckinsey.com/~/media/McKinsey/dotcom/client_service/ Organization/PDFs/Exec_Summ_WSJ_Preview_Special_Report.ashx

(30)   University of Kent research on 'The Role of Gender in Hiring Situations: The Preference for Potential'. Poster presentation to British Psychological Society Annual Conference in Liverpool 2015. https://www.science20.com/news_articles/in_hiring_simulation_male_potential_is_pre-ferred_over_a_female_track_record-155376

(31)   *How Much Can You Trust Your Brain? (2018). How It Works, Issue 118.*

(32)   *Moss-Racusin, C; Dovidio, JF; Brescoll, V; Graham, MJ; Handelsman, J. (2012). Science faculty's subtle gender biases favor male students. Proceedings of National Academy of Sciences USA. 2012 Oct 9;109(41)*

(33)   *Bohnet, I. (2016). What Works - Gender Equality by Design. The Belknap Press of Harvard University Press.*

(34)   *Reynolds, K. (2017). Women in business: advantages, challenges, and opportunities https://www.hult.edu/blog/women-in-business-advantages-challenges-and-opportunities/*

(35)   *Perry, Grayson. (2017). The Descent of Man. Penguin Books.*

(36)   *Buse, K. & Bilimoria. D. (2013). Women Who Persist. In SWE. p.45-51*

(37)   *Mohr, TS. (2014). Why Women Don't Apply for Jobs Unless They're 100% Qualified. Harvard Business Review, August 25, 2014.*

(38)   *Brands, R. & Fernandez-Mateo, I. (2017). Women Are Less Likely to Apply for Executive Roles If They've Been Rejected Before. Harvard Business Review. February 07, 2017. https://hbr.org/2017/02/women-are-less-likely-to-apply-for-executive-roles-if-theyve-been-rejected-before*

(39)   *Babcock, L. & Laschever, S. (2003). Women Don't Ask: Negotiation and the Gender Divide. Princeton University Press.*

(40)   *Ignatova, M. (2019) New Report: Women Apply to Fewer Jobs Than Men, But Are More Likely to Get Hired. https://business.linkedin.com/talent-solutions/blog/diversity/2019/how-women-find-jobs-gender-report*

(41)   *Dunbar, Angela. (2013): Solution to the 'Nine Dots' problem - thinking outside of the box. Last retrieved 2019-03-13 from https://www.youtube.com/watch?v=JOvjIAbB2i8*

(42)   *Insider (2020). Success isn't just about climbing the corporate ladder. Here's why 24 entrepreneurs quit their corporate jobs to start their own companies. https://www.businessinsider.com/women-who-left-corporate-jobs-to-start-their-own-companies-2020-11?r=US&IR=T*

(43)   *Reynolds, Katie. (2017). Women in business: advantages, challenges, and opportunities. https://www.hult.edu/blog/women-in-business-advantages-challenges-and-opportunities/*

(44)   *Annis, Barbara & Gray, John. (2016). Work With Me. How gender intelligence can help you succeed at work and at life. Piatkus.*

(45)   *Leanin.org*

(46)   *Johnson, SK. (2017). What 11 CEOs Have Learned About Championing Diversity. Harvard Business Review. August 17, 2017. UPDATED August 29, 2017.*

(47)   *Kelly, H. & Harlow, P. (2017). Salesforce CEO Marc Benioff's push for equality. CNNMoney (San Francisco) First published November 13, 2017.*

(48)   *Starbuck (2020). Our commitment to Inclusion, Diversity, and Equity at Starbucks. Oct 2020. https://stories.starbucks.com/stories/2020/our-commitment-to-inclusion-diversity-and-equity-at-starbucks/*

(49)   *Starbuck (2020). Workforce Diversity at Starbucks. Oct 2020. https://stories.starbucks.com/stories/2020/workforce-diversity-at-starbucks/*

(50)   *Need a Network of Champions. Why Mentoring & Sponsoring Are Important—Particularly for Women. https://www.ccl.org/articles/leading-effectively-articles/why-women-need-a-network-of-champions/*

(51)   Fitzgerald, Joy. (2018). How Lilly Is Getting More Women into Leadership Positions. Harvard Business Review, Oct 2018.

(52)   Office for National Statistics (2020). Gender pay gap in the UK: 2020. Differences in pay between women and men by age, region, full-time and part-time, and occupation. https://www.ons.gov.uk/employmentandlabourmarket/peopleinwork/earningsandworkinghours/bulletins/genderpaygapintheuk/2020

(53)   Schein, Edgar H. (1984). Coming to a New Awareness of Organizational Culture. Sloan Management Review, 25:2, 1984.

(54)   Wilson, Elisabeth M. (1998). Organisational culture as a framework for male and female progression and preferred management style. http://researchonline.ljmu.ac.uk/id/eprint/4992/1/285472.pdf

(55)   Mills, Albert & Murgatroyd, Stephen J. (1991). Organizational Rules: A framework for understanding organizational action. Open University Press, Milton Keynes.

(56)   Anon. (2019). I'm a female leader working in a boys club. This is what it's like. Women's Agenda. https://womensagenda.com.au/latest/im-a-female-leader-working-in-a-boys-club-this-is-what-its-like/

(57)   Marcus, Bonnie. (2015). The Politics of Promotion: How High Achieving Women Get Ahead and Stay Ahead. Wiley.

(58)   Nierenberg, S. (2008). Catalyst and Families and Work Institute; New Study Shows Gender, Rank, and Regional Differences in Finding the Right Fit for Top Corporate Talent. May 21, 2008. https://familiesandwork.org/downloads/FindingFitforTopTalent.pdf

(59)   Peterson, M. (2004). What men and women value at work: Implications for workplace health. Gender Medicine. December 2004.

(60)   Hahn, S. et al.(1995). Managing in the Age of Change: Essential Skills to Manage Today's Workforce.

(61)   Burns, J.M. (1978): Leadership. New York: Harper & Row

(62)   Bass, B. (1985): Leadership and Performance beyond expectations. New York: Free Press

(63)   Center for Creative Leadership. (2019). What Women Want From Work. https://www.ccl.org/blog/what-women-want-work/. February 24, 2019.

(64)   Mueller, H. (2018). 4 Excellent Examples of Diverse and Inclusive Company Cultures. https://emplify.com/blog/diversity-inclusion-culture-examples/

(65)   Boyatzis, R. (1982) The competent manager: A model for effective performance. New York: Wiley

(66)   Cannon, Kate. (2019). https://diademperformance.com/secret-emma-walmsleys-leadership-success/

(67)   Articles (2018). GlaxoSmithKline: Talking gender equality with pharma's first female CEO. https://www.vercida.com/uk/articles/gsk-first-female-ceo

(68)   Nikolova, Hristina & Cait Lamberton, Cait. (2016). Men Choose Differently When They Choose with Other Men. Harvard Business Review. September 14, 2016.

(69)   Clay, Cynthia. (2010) in Simpson, Corey. (2010). Are you maximizing team performance, on and off the field? https://www.comptia.org/blog/are_you_maximizing_team_performance_on_and_off_the_field.aspx

(70)   Cullinan, Renee. (2018). In Collaborative Work Cultures, Women Carry More of the Weight. Harvard Business Review. July 2018.

(71)   Dalai Lama (2012)., Interview in The Telegraph, 13 May 2012.

(72)   Malik, Fredmund. (2006). Führen Leisten Leben – Wirksames Management für eine neue Zeit. Frankfurt/Main: Campus Verlag GmbH.

(73)   Leanin.org. 7 Tips for Men Who Want to Support Equality.

(74)   Jay, Antony. (1976). How To Run a Meeting. Harvard Business Review. March 1976.

(75)   Raasted, Claus. (2020). Interview. THE COLLEGE OF EXTRAORDINARY EXPERIENCES. https://extraordinary.college/

(76)   Heider, F. (1958). The Psychology of Interpersonal Relations. New York: Wiley.

(77)   Pitts, A. (2013). You Only Have 7 Seconds To Make A Strong First Impression. Apr. 8, 2013. https://www.businessinsider.com/only-7-seconds-to-make-first-impression-2013-4?r=US&IR=T

(78)   Goleman, Daniel. (2000). Leadership that gets results. Harvard Business Review, 78 (2) 78-93, 2000.

(79)   Goleman, Daniel. (1995). Emotional Intelligence: Why It Can Matter More than IQ. New York: Bantam Books.

(80)   Goleman, D., Boyatzis, R., & McKee, A. (2002). Primal leadership: Realizing the power of emotional intelligence. Boston, MA: Harvard Business School Press.

(81)   Zenger, Jack. (2018). The Confidence Gap In Men And Women: Why It Matters And How To Overcome It. https://www.forbes.com/sites/jackzenger/2018/04/08/the-confidence-gap-in-men-and-women-why-it-matters-and-how-to-overcome-it/?sh=3e23d33e3bfa

(82)   Clance, Pauline & Imes, Suzanne. (1978). The imposter phenomenon in high achieving women: Dynamics and therapeutic intervention. Psychotherapy: Theory, Research & Practice, 15(3), 241–247, 1978.

(83)   Tulshyan, Ruchika & Burey, Jodi-Ann. (2021). Stop Telling Women They Have Imposter Syndrome. Harvard Business Review, Feb 2021.

(84)   Gerdeman, Dina. (2019). How Gender Stereotypes Kill a Woman's Self-Confidence. Harvard Business School Working Knowledge. https://hbswk.hbs.edu/item/how-gender-stereotypes-less-than-br-greater-than-kill-a-woman-s-less-than-br-greater-than-self-confidence

(85)   Axelrod, Ruth H. (2017). Leadership and Self-Confidence. Chapter 17 Leadership Today: Practices for Personal and Professional Performance, Joan Marques and Satinder Dhiman, eds., Springer.

(86)   McGee, Paul. (2005). SUMO. Capstone Publishing Ltd.

(87)   Scott, Sophie. (2020). How your brain works and how to make the most of it. New Scientist Academy.

(88)   Gruenfeld, D. (2013). Power & Influence. Mar 13, 2013. https://www.youtube.com/watch?v=K-dQHAeAnHmw

(89)   Ebersole, G. (2015). Dress for success: The importance of your workplace attire. March 2, 2015. https://www.readingeagle.com/business-weekly/article/dress-for-success-the-importance-of-your-workplace-attire

(90)   Zayas, V. (2016). Impressions Based on a Portrait Predict, 1-Month Later, Impressions Following a Live Interaction. Social Psychological and Personality Science 2016.

(91) Campbell, A. (2015). *Winners. And How They Succeed.* Penguin Random House UK.

(92) Mehrabian, Albert (1971). *Silent Messages.* Wadsworth Publishing Company Inc.

(93) Watzlawick, P. (1967). *Pragmatics of Human Communication: A Study of International Patterns, Pathologies, and Paradoxes.* W. W. Norton & Company.

(94) Peters, Tom. (1997). *The Brand Called You.* August 31, 1997. Fast Company Magazine.

(95) Obama, Michelle. (2018). *Becoming.* Penguin Random House Group.

(96) Sinek, Simon (2009). *Start with Why: How Great Leaders Inspire Everyone to Take Action.* Portfolio.

(97) McCafferty, N. (2009). *How not to dress for a job in the recession.* PUBLISHED July 27, 2009. https://www.express.co.uk/news/weird/116732/How-not-to-dress-for-a-job-in-the-recession

(98) George, Bill. et al. (2007). *Discovering Your Authentic Leadership.* Harvard Business Review 129, February 2007.

(99) Eichlinger, Bob & Lombardo, Mike (1996). *Coined the 70/20/10 formula from CCL research.* Source: CENTER FOR CREATIVE LEADERSHIP (n.d.): The 70-20-10 Rule for Leadership Development. https://www.ccl.org/articles/leading-effectively-articles/70-20-10-rule/

(100) Erpenbeck, J.; Von Rosenstiel, L. (2003). *Handbuch Kompetenzmessung.* Stuttgart: Schäffer-Poeschel.

(101) Tubbs, S. L., & Schulz, E. (2006). *Exploring a Taxonomy of Global Leadership Competencies and Meta-Competencies.* Journal of American Academy of Business, Cambridge, 8(2).

(102) Clutterbuck, D. & Schneider, S. (1998). *Executive mentoring.* Croner's Executive Companion. Bulletin, Issue 29, October.

(103) Shea, G. F. & Gianotti, S. C. (2009). *Mentoring – Make it a mutually rewarding experience.* 4th edition, Rochester.

(104) Bellevue University's Human Capital Lab (2010). *CASE STUDY: Sun Microsystems University Mentoring.* Source: https://www.hr.com/en/app/media/resource/_hcnvuvxk.deliver?s=tAtgX-EalqEbPc0euy&layout=og.pdf&mode=download.

(105) Allen, T.D., et al. (2004). *Career Benefits Associated With Mentoring for Proteges: A Meta-Analysis.* Journal of Applied Psychology 2004, Vol. 89, No. 1, 127–136

(106) Wharton University of Pennsylvania Report (2007). *Workplace Loyalties Change, but the Value of Mentoring Doesn't.* May 16, 2007. From https://knowledge.wharton.upenn.edu/article/workplace-loyalties-change-but-the-value-of-mentoring-doesnt/

(107) Bell, A. (2018). *Six rules for harnessing the power of a mentor.* Financial Times, March 6 2018. From https://www.ft.com/content/2ce849e0-10ad-11e8-a765-993b2440bd73

(108) Castrillon, Caroline. (2019). *Why Women Need To Network Differently Than Men To Get Ahead.* Forbes.com. https://www.forbes.com/sites/carolinecastrillon/2019/03/10/why-women-need-to-network-differently-than-men-to-get-ahead/?sh=19a69a6bb0a1

(109) de Janasz, S. C. & Forret, M. L. (2008). *Learning The Art of Networking: A Critical Skill for Enhancing Social Capital and Career Success.* Journal of Management Education. [Online] 32 (5).

(110) Granovetter, M. (1976). *Network sampling: Some first steps.* American journal of sociology, 81(6).

(111) Brown, E. (2011). *Strong and weak Ties: Why Your Weak Ties Matter.* SocialMediaToday. https://www.socialmediatoday.com/content/strong-andweak-ties-why-your-weak-ties-matter

(102)   Clark, D. (2016). Start Networking with People Outside Your Industry. Harvard Business Review. https://hbr.org/2016/10/start-networking-with-people-outside-yourindustry.

(113)   Roepe, Lisa R. (2018). The Hidden Networking Gao Between Men & Women. https://www.fastcompany.com/90277129/the-hidden-networking-gap-between-men-and-women

(114)   Uzzi, Brian. (2019). Research: Men and Women Need Different Kinds of Networks to Succeed. https://hbr.org/2019/02/research-men-and-women-need-different-kinds-of-networks-to-succeed

(115)   Andrews, Shaun. (2020). Why Women Don't Always Support Other Women. Forbes.com. https://www.forbes.com/sites/forbescoachescouncil/2020/01/21/why-women-dont-always-support-other-women/?sh=2c64922c3b05

(116)   Center for Creative Leadership. (2018). Women Pay a Price for Promoting Other Women. The Real Reason Behind "Queen Bee Syndrome". https://www.ccl.org/articles/leading-effectively-articles/queen-bee-women-pay-a-price-for-not-promoting-other-women/

(117)   Nazario, Brunilda. (2005). Why Men and Women Handle Stress Differently. WebMed June 06, 2005. https://www.webmd.com/women/features/stress-women-men-cope

(118)   Taylor SE, et al (2000). Biobehavioral responses to stress in females: Tend-and-befriend, not fight-or-flight. Psychological Review. 2000;107(3):411-429.

(119)   Gross, Gail. (2013). How Men Handle Stress Differently. Huffpost Blog 06/18/2013. https://www.huffpost.com/entry/men-and-stress_b_3430607

(120)   Selye, H. (1956). The Stress of Life. New York: McGraw-Hill.

(121)   Lazarus, R.S. (1966). Psychological Stress and the Coping Process. New York: McGraw-Hill.

(122)   Rampe, M. (2010). Der R-Faktor. Hamburg & Norderstedt: Books on Demand GmbH.

(123)   Lufkin, Brian. (2021). Is the formal "suited and booted" office dress code extinct? BBC. https://www.bbc.com/worklife/article/20210713-is-the-formal-suited-and-booted-office-dress-code-extinct

ACKNOWLEDGEMENTS

Our passion for working with and developing women in business and leadership stems from having had the privilege of working with many great leaders, both women and men, but having had the pleasure of being part of many women's journeys of self-discovery and learning to be the best they can be. Progress can be hard. For many women, it is a juggling act, or it means making compromises. The rewards when women make it to the top are immense though, for the individuals and for their colleagues and wider networks. We are honoured to work with these incredible women who strive hard every day to make a difference. Thank you to all of you as you have inspired us to write this book.

We also want to thank our own mentors, sponsors and champions who supported us along our career journeys. We have only done what we have done because of them. In our network, there have been a great number of inspirational and loyal men who have shaped our learning, opened doors for us and given advice or simple encouragement when we needed it the most. Our heartfelt thanks for all this support go to Prof. Dr. Heinz Mandl, Thomas Schweins, Peer Schatz, Hans Peter Fatscher, Hauke Dirk Jacob and Richard Lidbetter.

We want to specially thank Sabine Decker. Sabine inspires many women and sponsors many more in their leadership development. She is an incredible role model for team success and a personal learning journey. To Ian Roberts, we are honoured to have your support and encouragement and wholeheartedly wish you success with your vision at the university.

To our champions Ashley Bird, Line Raquet and Marie Krstic, a big thank you for believing in our approach to leadership. Not only are you true role models, but your willingness to challenge us and your abilities to make sense of complexity, provide new perspectives and guide positive outcomes have ensured that we all keep learning and growing, both personally and professionally.

To our proof-readers Emma Caldwell, Barry Barnes and Rose Grayson, we extend a massive thank you for your time and diligence to review our message, our flow and our spelling! It is your inputs that enable us to share our concepts in a positive way that others can also enjoy them more. Many others have also generously shared their time, including Sophie Grayson, Chantal Vandevorst and Russell Dean. We are extremely grateful for all their support.

Finally, thank you to Alison Stoker for reminding us that, by using techniques such as yoga, we can develop our minds and build our integrity and as we do so, we are able to expand our compassion. May we all follow our dreams and live each day with the courage to keep going, the curiosity to keep challenging and kindness to create a more inclusive world.

Other Books by Katrin Winkler & Nicola Bramwell:

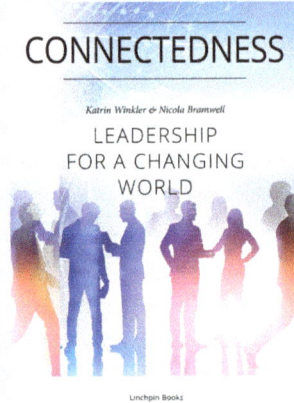

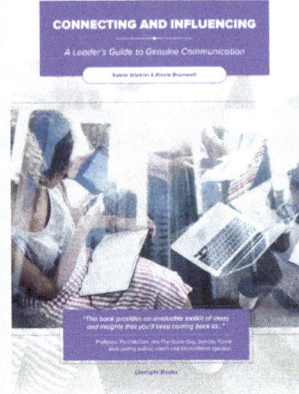

"CONNECTEDNESS: **LEADERSHIP FOR A CHANGING WORLD**"

This book considers how leaders can connect by caring, inspiring, appreciating, developing and empowering. It considers how balance can be achieved between doing the right thing for the business (effective management) and doing them in the right way for people (leadership principles). By establishing a transformational environment for teams, projects or organizations, our human need to contribute and succeed can be harnessed. What is different is the shift from a traditional, hierarchic notion of control to values of trust and fulfilment that can be applied equally well in small teams, virtual teams and global corporations. This shift can also be applied equally well by individual managers, project leaders or senior executives with the desire and imagination to create a shared sense of purpose.

ISBN: 9789464075410 - www.linchpinbooks.eu

"CONNECTING AND INFLUENCING:
A LEADER'S GUIDE TO GENUINE COMMUNICATION"

Designed as a compendium, this book looks at communication knowledge, skills, mindset and tools, and refreshes application of useful models. It aims to challenge individuals to choose to care about how they communicate and positively influence others by considering why communication is so important, what mindset is needed to make a difference and then the right tool or approach for different work-related scenarios including the virtual world. It is about the goal and the meaning conveyed when you set out to share information, seek input, discuss ideas, build relationships, show appreciation, or open up about hopes and dreams. By combining real-life examples, theory and practical application, we share valuable and highly applicable know-how so readers can grow as communicators and have a reliable resource to go back to time and time again.

ISBN: 9789464075427 - www.linchpinbooks.eu

INDEX OF KEY TERMS

Lightning Source UK Ltd.
Milton Keynes UK
UKHW022055041221
395049UK00003B/38